Maria Morozova-Duthoit brings a blend of sales expertise and marketing wisdom honed over two decades of leadership in deal-making and client relationships. Her strategic acumen has been pivotal at top advertising agencies like Leo Burnett, McCann Erickson and BBDO, helping world-famous brands achieve new levels of success. At Google, Maria led advertising sales teams working on the company's largest clients, fuelling exponential growth across multi-million-dollar accounts and fostering lasting client relationships. Now, as Managing Partner at Catalyst, she focuses on consulting, sales training and executive coaching, specialising in building super teams and driving commercial results. With an International Executive MBA from HEC Paris, her insights into business dynamics are penetrating and actionable. Passionate about revealing the untapped potential of businesses and people, Maria is widely recognised by clients and colleagues for catalysing profound change in those organisations she leads.

David Kean is an author, keynote speaker, entrepreneur and energiser. For over three decades, tens of thousands of business people all over the world have enjoyed the excitement and energy of David's events on personal performance and persuasion, pitching, sales, negotiation and leadership. David has helped business leaders to win millions in new revenues and extract the highest performance from themselves and their teams. Clients have described David's work with them as 'game-changing' – even 'life-changing'. David is co-founder of the management consultancy Catalyst. Catalyst helps change the way organisations think, align, communicate and take action around the issue of business growth and work with both start-ups and multinationals across multiple industries, from fashion and technology to automotive and professional services.

T0299649

THE
WORK
SMARTER
GUIDE TO
SALES

Maria Morozova-Duthoit
& David Kean

Series Editor David Kean

A How To book

ROBINSON

ROBINSON

First published in Great Britain in 2024
by Robinson.

10 9 8 7 6 5 4 3 2 1

A CIP catalogue record for this book
is available from the British Library.

ISBN: 978-1-47214-890-2

Typeset in Sentinel and Scala Sans
by Ian Hughes.

Printed and bound in Great Britain by Clays
Ltd, Elcograf S.p.A.

Papers used by Robinson are from well-
managed forests and other responsible
sources.

MIX
Paper | Supporting
responsible forestry
FSC® C104740

Robinson
An imprint of
Little, Brown Book Group
Carmelite House
50 Victoria Embankment
London EC4Y 0DZ

An Hachette UK Company
www.hachette.co.uk

www.littlebrown.co.uk

How To Books are published by
Robinson, an imprint of Little, Brown
Book Group. We welcome proposals
from authors who have first-hand
experience of their subjects. Please set
out the aims of your book, its target
market and its suggested contents in an
email to howto@littlebrown.co.uk.

Acknowledgements

Every client and colleague we've ever worked with and learnt from but in particular: Simon Thomas; Dame Annette King, DBE; Miles Young; Jose Neves; Paul Simons; Sophie Devonshire; Phil Gripton; Myriam Vander Elst; Glen Lomas; Stephen Maher; Stuart Archibald; Kevin Kroggman; Julia Anfilova; Evgenia Brodskaya; Tatiana Maslova; Hetal Gordon; Natalia Ignatovich; Igor Kirikchi.

Contents

Introduction

*'If people like you, they'll listen to you, but if they trust you,
they'll do business with you.'*
ZIG ZIGLAR, AUTHOR AND SALES EXECUTIVE

You're a castaway on an island with people you don't know. You need to agree on who will lead the group. Everyone agrees the leader should be trustworthy, but all you have to go on is the profession of each candidate.

Who do you vote for?

The doctor?

The accountant?

The professional musician?

The salesperson?

If you're like most people, you came up with the doctor, the accountant, the musician and the salesperson – in that order. According to a survey from HubSpot Research, 49 per cent of people trust doctors, 12 per cent trust accountants, 10 per cent trust professional musicians. Only 3 per cent of people trust salespeople.

Even though selling is the engine that keeps all economies moving and can be traced all the way back to the Silk Road, *The Arabian Nights* and exotic places such as Istanbul's Grand Bazaar, many people still don't feel comfortable being described as a salesperson. Which is a shame. Because serving people's needs and wants is that most human of activities and it's been around for as long as humankind itself. Selling is an art form handed down from generation to generation, and being good at it transforms your personal success and turbo-charges your business's performance.

The two of us, Maria and David, have been in the sales game for ages – and not just any sales: advertising sales. The sharpest end of the persuasion game. Our mission is to restore some dignity to this age-old skill and to show how it is the progenitor of all business activity. After all, *nothing happens until someone sells something.*

How to use this book

In this book, we simplify the art of selling so you can put it to work quickly for yourself, your team and your business. As it says on the front cover, this book is a guide to help make your selling superb. We aim to help you sell smarter and to supercharge the results you achieve. The skills in this book will work in a multitude of situations: leading a team, fundraising, public speaking, interviewing for a job, consulting, mentoring, parenting and many more. The investment of your effort in the programme will pay dividends in many aspects of your life.

The philosophy in this guide isn't to put on a slick suit, shiny shoes, a dazzling smile and to go out into the world spreading bullshit. There's too much of that already. We are talking about a whole different style of selling. We want to help you be the best of the breed, which means you sell using your own unique set of strengths and bring your own unique flavour to every client you meet. You bring them the very best of yourself and your objective is dead simple: to help them achieve their objectives. We can only make you into the best salesperson you can be if we do it *your* way. The way you sell has to be authentic to who you are and how you work. Which is why this guide is 'interactive'. To get the most out of it requires you to work too. We recommend that you set aside time every day over the next five weeks to work on the programme; we'll even show you how to make the time to dedicate to it. The more you put into the next five weeks, the more you will get out of them.

Together, we'll work through the core skills of selling and tailor them to your unique personality and circumstances. At the end of our journey together you'll be equipped to:

- Understand what selling really is, and what it isn't
- Sell in the way that is most suited to your unique personality
- Build quick and deep rapport with potential clients and customers
- Win clients' minds
- Win clients' hearts
- Help your clients make better decisions
- Be systematic in your approach
- Generate better results on an ongoing basis
- Create a solid game plan to skyrocket your business.

Let's get started

We assume that you are aiming to grow your business and develop professionally. But what exactly will it mean for you to be a better salesperson? Whether you are just starting out or you are already a seasoned professional, it's essential to ascertain what you expect for yourself and from this programme.

Spend a few minutes writing down your goals in the context of your existing situation. These could be goals directly connected to your business performance, for example expanding your customer base by x per cent, doubling your average contract size or winning five new clients in the next twelve months. They could also be your personal and professional growth goals: to get a pay rise within the next six months, to expand your relationship with your largest client and work for a new division of their company, to increase your self-confidence or to get your board's buy-in to a big new initiative.

Goals: _____

_____

_____

_____

_____

_____

_____

_____

_____

_____

_____

For every goal that you come up with, ask yourself:

1. Does this goal fulfil the **SMART** criteria? Is it:
Specific and **M**easurable with clear outcomes
Achievable with set actions
Relevant to your personal and professional growth in sales and persuasion
Time-bound with set deadlines?
2. Do the outcomes depend on you? Even if you are the manager of a team, whose performance you would like to improve, the goal should focus on *your own* change and necessary actions, not on those of your team members.
3. How will you know you are moving in the right direction and that you have achieved your goal with tangible evidence? How will other people acknowledge it?

During our five weeks together, always relate what we say back to your own personal goals. As we progress, you might revise your goals, re-prioritise them or add more to the list. But always keep your goals in mind throughout the work. Do this and you will extract from the programme what is of most relevance and benefit to *you*.

Losing sight of your goals is like sailing without a compass: you might continue moving, but you are unlikely to reach your desired destination.

Happy selling!

Week One:
You

'I don't sell. What I do is help people with their problems'
SMALL BUSINESS OWNER

Your beliefs about sales and selling

Most people don't want to be seen as salespeople. Salespeople are always *other* people. A special group possessing certain traits: innate persuasive talent, natural charisma and the gift of the gab. More negatively, those traits might include being manipulative and pushy. We often have strong opinions about them:

> 'Sales is only for extroverts'
> 'She can sell sand in a desert'
> 'Stay alert if you don't want to be wrapped around his finger'

We asked people on LinkedIn for their immediate associations with sales and selling. Here are the positives:

+ Storyteller
+ Reliable partner
+ A bridge between the company and customers
+ Relationship builder
+ Ambassador
+ Influencer

Here are the negatives:

- Someone extremely annoying, too direct, too unsophisticated
- A person eager and willing to talk you into *anything*
- Someone who won't take 'no' as an answer
- Tricky rascal
- Manipulative
- Oily
- Only interested in making a sale.

And our favourite one: 'short-term best friend'!

Even if you can't articulate your feelings precisely, salespeople still get labelled. A friend of ours, Mariella, dedicated her life to building a corporate career in marketing. One day Mariella decided to launch her own advertising agency. The aspect that made her worry most was having to go out and sell. She told us that at the start, when she had no capital or income, she was going to take care of everything except sales. For that, she was going to hire a specialist.

'Why would you hire a salesperson?', we asked. 'You know so much about advertising. You're a marketer with an impressive track record. You've got plenty to say and loads of contacts in the client world.' But she didn't think she could do the things that salespeople do: 'I'm not a salesperson!'

'Good!', we said. 'Make that the hook in your sales process. Tell people you're not a salesperson, but that you know a thing or two about the issues clients face and that you're here to find out how you might be able to help.'

Years later, our friend told us that this introduction always worked as the perfect ice-breaker: her open and genuine manner plus her helpful attitude were a winning combination. She stumbled across a great truth about *real* selling and salespeople: they have knowledge which is useful, and they put helping before selling.

The currency of selling is generosity – seeking to serve someone else's agenda, not your own.

If people think you are only out for yourself, they will spot you coming a mile away and run for the hills. Don't be *that* sort of salesperson. Instead, be like our friend, Mariella: stop selling, start helping.

Let's get into your own beliefs about selling. Write down your top-of-mind thoughts and associations about salespeople, both positive and negative. Start with:

The majority of salespeople are . . .

1/ _____

2/ _____

3/ _____

Now that you have them, work on each one and answer these three questions:

1/ Where does this belief come from? Have I ever met a salesperson that was not like this and still successful?

_____

_____

_____

2/ What are the benefits and risks of me keeping this attitude towards salespeople as I endeavour to become a better salesperson?

_____

_____

_____

3/ How can I change my beliefs so they can help me rather than hinder me?

_____

_____

_____

1/ Where does this belief come from? Have I ever met a salesperson that was not like this and still successful?
If your associations are negative, you're probably thinking of used car salespeople, timeshare hustlers or cold callers – people (or AI programs) who bombard you with messages, trap you into talking and use aggressive tactics to twist you into committing time and maybe money. These are people we naturally shy away from – people we feel prey on the vulnerable or take advantage of our good nature when we don't want to appear rude. They often exploit a lack of knowledge about the category or product that is being sold. They often use arguments and evidence that are hard to validate.

This is, sadly, the stereotype. They are really just rip-off merchants, not sales professionals. We don't want anything to do with them or the tactics they employ.

If you thought of someone who was *not* like the stereotype, but was still successful, you probably met someone who was reliable, behaved honestly and was authentic. This is what we mean by a professional salesperson. Neither a 'natural born hunter', nor someone who is just nice. We mean a person who is genuinely trying to help someone else – a client – to solve a problem. A person who makes the effort to find out the client's challenges and aspirations, who understands how their product or service can help, and who proves they are trustworthy throughout the relationship by offering honest advice.

In short, you met someone who builds relationships not just transactions. Who serves their own interest by serving those of their client and who is positive, encouraging and, above all else, helpful.

2/ How do I benefit and what do I risk, keeping this attitude towards salespeople?
There are many beliefs in life that we simply don't question. Most of them are not truly our opinions, but social conditioning dictated by parents or peer groups. Such stereotypes might save time by making

proper reflection unnecessary (which is often helpful), but some limit us by creating a rigid mindset. Our brain protects us from stepping into the unknown or trying new things and opts for the safety of the status quo.

When you have the objective of becoming a good salesperson but carry around in your head a lazy, negative stereotype, you need to reframe how you see selling and how you see yourself as a salesperson, or else you will be fighting your own belief system. There's a concept invented by the psychologist Edward de Bono called 'rivers of thinking'. Just as rivers flow down established paths, so do our attitudes and thoughts. Our biases, background and conditioning create mental grooves that shape our thinking and behaviour. If we don't challenge our own preconceptions, we risk missing new perspectives, ideas and opportunities for personal growth.

Look at your list of associations with salespeople and ask yourself: what works to my advantage, and what will impede my development?

3/ How can I change my beliefs so they help rather than hinder?

Our brains are adaptable and capable of change – it's called neuroplasticity. We can consciously develop new ways of thinking, behaving and responding. Now that you have identified any limiting beliefs around the subject of selling, how can you reformulate your beliefs positively to support your progress on this programme? How can you change the course of the rivers of your thinking?

Answer: by formulating your own approach to selling so that it feels natural to *you*. Which means we need to understand how you see yourself and how others see you.

'To know thyself is the beginning of wisdom'
SOCRATES

Let's begin with an analysis of you through two lenses:

- your own perception of yourself
- other people's perceptions of you.

How you see yourself

There is a very useful and practical way of evaluating your strengths and weaknesses which will also help you to understand your behavioural style – **personality profiling**. There are numerous personality profiling methodologies from MBTI to DISC. You can use any you like. We will use a very simple and practical one: social styles. We like things to be simple and useful – this one is the simplest and, we believe, the best. Let's give it a go. You are going to answer fourteen questions. It shouldn't take more than ten minutes to do this exercise.

- Each question gives you a choice between two alternatives.
- Choose the alternative that you believe is more true to you. You must choose *one*.
- Circle your answer to each question.

Don't overthink the answers. This questionnaire is designed to reveal to you your *dominant* social style.

Here we go.

1. Which is more important to you?

Being in charge of something	Top
Working in a team	Bottom

2. Do you prefer?

To tell people what you did at the weekend	Right
To listen to what they did	Left

3. What would you rather do?

Take part in your favourite hobby	Top
Meet somebody famous you admire	Bottom

4. Which kind of people do you prefer?

Confident, lively people	Right
Modest, easy-going people	Left

5. Do you consider yourself to be?

A rational person	Top
An emotional person	Bottom

6. How well do you accept criticism?

Accept it fairly happily	Right
Hate to get criticism	Left

7. Which do you think is more important in life?

Your knowledge and expertise	Top
Your ability to get on with people	Bottom

8. Which are you more likely to do?

To make a quick decision and just go for it	Right
To make planned and considered decisions	Left

9. Are you more comfortable?

On your own or in a small group	Top
In large groups	Bottom

10. Which do you agree most with?

I trust my instincts and judgement	Right
I like to research and read reviews before I buy things	Left

11. Which do you agree most with?

I think my work life and social life will be separate	Top
My work life and social life will greatly overlap	Bottom

12. Which do you agree most with?

Success comes from inspiration and leadership	Right
Success comes from teamwork and unity of purpose	Left

13. Do you?

Never discuss feelings	Top
Talk easily about your feelings	Bottom

14. Do you?

Like luxury and well-known brands	Right
Fashion brands do not matter that much to you	Left

- Count up whether you have more *Rights* or *Lefts*
- Count whether you have more *Bottoms* or *Tops*
- *Which quadrant are you in?*

TOP LEFT	TOP RIGHT
BOTTOM LEFT	BOTTOM RIGHT

Let us explain how it works.

Locate yourself on the chart below.

TASK

S L O W	Slow/Task (Analytical)	Fast/Task (Driver)	F A S T
	Slow/Relationship (Amiable)	Fast/Relationship (Expressive)	

RELATIONSHIP

This matrix divides people into those who are more *task oriented* and those who are more *relationship oriented*. It then further categorises people by whether they feel more comfortable *operating at speed* or at a *more deliberative, slower pace*. The quadrant you inhabit determines your **dominant** behavioural style.

If you are:
TOP LEFT: you are an *Analytical* – slow, task-oriented
TOP RIGHT: you are a *Driver* – fast, task-oriented
BOTTOM LEFT: you are an *Amiable* – slow, relationship-oriented
BOTTOM RIGHT: you are an *Expressive* – fast, relationship-oriented

Another way of describing these dynamics is that those on the left-hand side of the matrix like to think before they talk and often prefer listening before speaking. Those on the right-hand side of the matrix often *talk in order to think* and tend to 'tell' rather than ask.

It is important to say that most people have traits of all four. It is highly likely that you had at least one answer from the left even if all the others were on the right. It might be that your answers split between top and bottom pretty evenly – but if one of them outnumbers the other, that's your dominant behavioural style. Most people have some elements of all four quadrants. This is perfectly normal and very useful in life. It shows us that we are flexible and capable of using different behavioural styles – the same way as we can wear all sorts of different clothes even if we feel particularly comfortable with a specific 'look'. So you may find something in your behaviour that resonates with each style. However, if you are honest with yourself, one of these styles will be closer to you and you will be able to recognise yourself.

Why is it important? Because the better we understand ourselves the better we will be able to see what image we produce for different people and in different circumstances.

So, who are you?

TOP LEFT – Analytical

Analytical people prioritise getting things right. For you the most important thing is *not* to make mistakes. You also think it is important to explain how you or someone else arrived at an objective solution or decision. You like detail and mistrust flashiness or flamboyance.

You probably see yourself as precise, careful, reserved and logical.

But can you guess how all of these wonderful qualities can be seen by others, who are not in your style (particularly on a bad day)? They may see you as stubborn, nit-picking, pedantic, unemotional and negative.

Can you see how conflict would arise very quickly in an interaction between an Analytical person and someone who doesn't see the world like they do: an Expressive.

BOTTOM RIGHT – Expressive

Expressives are diametrically opposite to Analyticals on the matrix – bottom right versus top left. And they behave in the opposite way, too. Expressives are like human potassium. Can you remember the chemistry experiment from school where you take a piece of potassium and place it onto water? You get fireworks – the potassium melts and fizzes around very quickly on the surface of the water, self-ignites and releases hydrogen gas which results in sparks and a lilac flame. Spectacular.

If you are an Expressive, you are likely to be like this – someone who is excitable, enjoys company, is full of creative ideas and innovation. You are energetic, open, optimistic and fast. And when you are in the company of other Expressives, the noise and energy levels go through the roof!

Expressives' biggest insecurities are being ignored and missing out.

You are often seen by others who are not like you as pushy, superficial, overconfident – as people who exaggerate and don't follow through with commitments.

TOP RIGHT – Driver

Drivers prioritise *getting things done*. You are action-oriented – like the Nike slogan of 'Just do it' but in human form. You like to feel in charge and hate any loss of control. You may be good at delegating work but not decisions. You see your goal and drive towards it no matter what. You probably see yourself as exacting, efficient, determined, decisive and direct.

But others can see you as autocratic, critical, demanding, insensitive and domineering.

This style is diametrically opposite that of Amiables (top right versus bottom left), and you can alienate people by riding rough-shod over others.

BOTTOM LEFT – Amiables

Amiables are life's diplomats. Your focus is the wellbeing of the team, and your priority is to build consensus between everyone. You avoid conflict and see yourself as warm, accepting, patient, cooperative and friendly.

But you are often seen by others, who are not in your behavioural style group, as weak, lacking goals, slow to make decisions or take responsibility and a time-waster.

Your strength is that you will never try to gain short-term advantage at the expense of the long-term relationship. Consequently, you are often more trusted than the other groups.

However, the truth is that each of us contains elements of all four personality styles in our own combination. This is what makes us unique. On top of that, we must avoid stereotypes.

A Driver may be an extremely caring person but express that care with practical advice and help. If you are also a Driver, you are likely to understand and appreciate this. However, if you are an Amiable, you will probably exhibit a caring attitude by asking everyone's opinion, making sure everyone feels comfortable and safe, and that their personal needs are taken into account. But that style of caring may be misinterpreted by a Driver as wasting time, when what they really want is advice and help!

Expressives do not spend less time *thinking* than Analytical people – they just go about it in a different way. Analytical people can be very creative, but it looks and feels different to the way Expressive people demonstrate their creativity.

Write down below how you would describe yourself.
Think of your behaviour at work when you are calm and when you are under stress. Think of your interaction with others – colleagues, clients, bosses, peers, those who report to you. Be honest, neither too complimentary nor too dismissive.

It might help if you imagine yourself from the perspective of a different person. Listen to yourself and capture your perception:

- How does it feel to be in the company of this person (you!)?
- Is this person trustworthy?
- Is this person persuasive?
- How do they interact with other people?
- How would you describe this person's image: style of clothing, voice, manners, posture, physiology, personality?
- Do they appear calm or nervous, open or closed, friendly or grumpy?
- Imagine you are in the airport and your flight is delayed for several hours. What would it be like to spend time in the company of this person? What might you enjoy? What might you find challenging?

How I describe myself _____

_____

_____

_____

_____

_____

_____

_____

How others see you

Ask five colleagues and friends that you trust to share their perceptions of you. Read through any evaluation forms or 360 assessments you have from work. You are looking for a rounded picture of how you come across to others. Areas to probe:

- What are my key strengths when I interact with other people?
- How well do I adapt my communication style to different people and different situations?
- When in a one-on-one conversation with me, do I make you feel understood, valued and convinced about my ideas?
- How would you describe the impression that I create in group settings?
- What would you suggest I do to improve my communication skills?
- Any other observations in relation to how I come across to others?

Now that you have your own notes and third-party feedback, it's time to analyse the data. Review the responses and identify common themes, any patterns or contradictory points and any areas for improvement.

Other people's perception of you

_____

_____

_____

_____

_____

_____

_____

For some people there is a significant difference between their perception of themselves and the perception others have of them. If that's the case for you, try not to engage with the data you've collected in an emotional way. Instead, approach it in a non-judgemental way: at the moment you're at point A. We want to get to point B in five weeks' time. By point B, you will have greatly increased your self-awareness and self-confidence and be a better salesperson. Analyse the data objectively, as if you are a top athlete deconstructing your technique. For example, when top tennis players are interviewed after a big match, they always talk about their game objectively: 'the backhand wasn't working as well as usual today'; 'I need to work on the approach to net more in order to get a faster return'; 'I need physio and weight training to strengthen the muscles around that injured wrist'. They assess their performance and how best to improve it without judgement. They don't beat themselves up for being a bad player.

Do not beat yourself up; simply play to your strengths and be aware of any weaknesses.

Understanding why you behave in a certain way helps you adjust to different people without feeling schizophrenic. Let's look at the most common strength and weakness for each style and how you can help yourself to adjust.

Analytical. Your weakness is speed of decision-making, because you need time and data and do not want to be caught unprepared or propose solutions which come out of the blue. Our advice is *not* to simply rely on your intuition or be more like Drivers and Expressives.

Do not be bullied into making quick solutions; just buy yourself time. Do not start 'thinking out loud' with Drivers and Expressives; simply state that you need to think and ask for an extra five minutes/hours/weeks. You can also buy time when you ask for more information, detail or for clarification – you are good at asking questions, so use that skill.

Expressive. Your brilliant fountain of ideas becomes a weakness when another person needs a structured, step-by-step description of the idea. Prepare it beforehand. Have that 300-page presentation up your sleeve. Do not try to be Analytical and present it. You will fail. Remain Expressive and charm them; think out loud and see how they respond – entertain them. But give them the deck so that they can read it when you are gone.

Driver. You do not listen and you fight any objections to your proposal. So you often run the risk of *winning the argument but losing the sale.* As a goal-oriented Driver, keep reminding yourself that your goal is a good relationship with your client. Your goal is not to prove that you are right. Such a goal will only give you a Pyrrhic victory.

Amiable. You are brilliant at building long-term relationships but may get stuck in endless discussions that do not result in any sales. We are not asking you to be more determined and decisive. Instead, use your strength of caring for the comfort of people around you and throw the ball to your client – suggest that they should make a decision on the next step. A Driver and an Expressive will be happy to make it there and then. An Analytical will ask for time to think – just do not forget to agree on a specific date when they will come back with their decision.

Now that you have reframed the way you view selling and salespeople, and have reflected on how you perceive yourself and how others perceive you, it's time to outline your personal brand image, presentation style and sales approach.

Using your unique skills to sell your way

What are you good at and how can you help others?

Let's identify and use your core talents to create your own unique approach to selling. Too many people dismiss their own talents, often because these abilities come so naturally to them that they take them for granted. We encounter many individuals who genuinely believe that what they excel at is something anyone can do. Here's the key insight: *skills and talents that come effortlessly to you may not be so straightforward for others.* You'd be amazed at how others often look on in admiration at what you do that they cannot do.

We've observed a variety of traits people often overlook:

- detailed information-gathering and astute analysis
- seeing the bigger picture
- getting on with all types of people
- bringing different and unusual perspectives to problems
- quick to assimilate lots of information
- brilliant at building consensus.

Remember: every trait is valuable, so do not downplay or dismiss any of yours. In combination, they are the talents that you, uniquely, offer the world and they must be put to work in the way you sell.

Because of this inability to value our own talents, we ignore them and invest all our faith in external factors: job titles, roles and professional qualifications. These become our personal brand image – but they are not anchored in ourselves. Such an approach is dangerous. Identifying your self-worth solely by job title or the status of the company you work for can leave you very vulnerable. If you are made redundant, move location or take a career break, all sense of self-identity will evaporate with the last pay cheque. You have to redefine your own sense of self independently of the company payroll.

As we discovered by looking at different behavioural styles, the qualities that make you shine are often the same as those that cause problems for you. For example, quick thinkers will have a tendency to rush. Empathetic people may struggle to be decisive.

Let's examine your core skills.

Think of five experiences from your work, personal or academic life when you achieved something that was significant for you. Perhaps you mastered a new skill, overcame a particular challenge or were truly proud of yourself. Ask yourself:

- What *exactly* did you excel at within the story?
- How did you triumph/tackle the challenge/improve the situation?
- Which of your skills/talents played a key role in achieving this outcome?

Experience: _____

_____

_____

Learning: _____
Experience: _____

_____

_____

Learning: _____
Experience: _____

_____

_____

Learning: _____
Experience: _____

_____

_____

Learning: _____

Experience: _____
_____
_____

Learning: _____

Look for patterns – these are your core skills.

Skills: _____
_____
_____
_____
_____

Think how you can use these strengths to fashion *your own* selling style. In many ways, you are selling yourself – so it's important to be clear on the self you are selling. If you thought that effective salespeople all possessed the same traits, think again.

Acknowledging and using your unique skills will give you confidence and amplify your personal energy. Why? Because you are acting *authentically* – using your own natural talents. Which makes it easy because you're pushing *with* the grain rather than against it.

Creating your personal brand image

Let's look at the way you present yourself to the world – your physiology, the way you dress, your voice, manners and the energy you project. When you interact with others, they are constantly evaluating you, often on an unconscious level. Let's delve into the five key dimensions of interpersonal perception so you can fine-tune each one to create your desired personal brand image:

1. **Visual:** Your appearance and choice of attire
2. **Kinaesthetic:** The way you move and your body language
3. **Auditory:** The tone, pitch and intonation of your voice

4. Semantic: The narratives you share and whether your words resonate
5. Energy: How others feel about you, your 'likeability'

VISUAL

Humans have always judged one another based on appearance. The way you look – from hairstyle and skin to clothes and accessories. In many cases people make the wrong assumptions. But they still make them. You cannot prevent others from making assumptions. The brain is designed to make assumptions within several seconds of seeing another person. This is simply our biological survival mechanism.

Knowing this, salespeople need to think carefully about the visual impression they make. Some professions have a defined dress code to signal authority or reliability or experience – imagine passengers' unease if an airline pilot arrived on the flight deck dressed in worn-out jeans and a T-shirt. If you're in a profession where there are dress codes, that makes it easy.

For many, dress codes are liberalising. What guidelines are there when, for many businesspeople, anything goes? We quite like the admonition given by Google's co-founder, Larry Page, when asked what his company's dress code was: *'You must wear something.'*

But we propose a more nuanced viewpoint. When you're a salesperson engaging directly with clients, there are two things to consider:

1. Your attire should be a reflection of your personality, something that makes *you feel you;*
2. The context and the audience.

People usually make mistakes in their choice of attire due to their personality style.

- Amiables often underdress for the occasion. They look too cosy, too relaxed, too 'domestic'. Because they want to feel at ease, they think casual is okay. Sometimes that attitude can cost.
- Expressives meeting Analyticals may appear showy or flamboyant.
- Analyticals can sometimes look like they got dressed in the dark – nothing matches and they can look a little unkempt.
- Drivers are normally neat and tidy. Those who don't conform to a Driver's own, stringent dress codes will be quickly judged.

Silicon Valley company founders may wear T-shirts and flip-flops to their office but they dress differently when they attend a Congressional hearing.

If all else fails, go for a classic look if you're meeting someone for the first time. Then at least you won't offend anyone. As a rule, wear simple clothes but don't wear cheap clothes.

Write down three adjectives you hope other people would use to describe your personal style. Whether you lean towards 'elegant', 'bold', 'unconventional' or 'disciplined', let these terms guide your fashion choices.

_____

_____

_____

KINAESTHETIC

Everyone recognises the importance of body language. But only a few dedicate time to use it or remain conscious of their own movements – and other's movements – during client meetings or presentations. But it is essential in selling to be aware of body language, because it conveys information that helps you steer your sales conversation with a client in the right direction.

Body language focuses on the space you occupy and the confidence you exude. It is part of our evolutionary make-up. For instance:

- Individuals who sit on the edge of their chairs in a closed pose, which makes the body smaller to make it less of a target, are signalling stress, discomfort and a desire to 'get outta here'. It's reminiscent of how small prey animals behave when sensing danger: staying low, aiming to be nearly invisible. Emitting such non-verbal cues to others in a room is rarely to one's advantage.
- Overly dominant behaviour, akin to an alpha male or silverback gorilla – constantly demonstrating power and authority – can repel others. The famous handshake of President Trump is an example of that. (Check it out on YouTube.) It just ends up making you look like you're trying too hard.

Nowadays, we need to be aware of our own and other's body language not just face to face but online as well. Online, body language mistakes are much more noticeable than in real life. In an online call, our brain suffers from the very limited amount of visual information it is getting on the 15-inch screen. So it grabs anything it can get.

Common mistakes people make online

Mistake

Poor eye contact. It's particularly difficult when you are talking to a screen with many participants and do not know which one to look at.

Remedy

Don't use two screens. If you have to read something, put it in front of you, not on a different screen. You can also put a toy or someone's photo next to the camera to create 'in the room presence' and talk to this toy/person on your desk rather than to 10 little screens of your online conference.

Mistake

Too little movement or too much movement.

Remedy

If we can't tell whether you are alive, maybe lean in a little and help us see that you're engaged. Hold on to a pen to give your hands something to do and don't sit on a swivel chair!

Mistake

Touching face and hair.

Remedy

Try the 'holding the pen' trick again. Rest your chin on your hand – and keep it there!

Mistake

Being too close to the screen makes you appear a bit threatening. Conversely, being too far away from the screen makes you look aloof, disengaged and uninvolved.

Remedy

Get your camera at eye level so we don't have to look up your nose or down on the top of your head. Sit up comfortably – don't lean in on your arms so you loom too large on the screen. Equally, don't have your chair so far away from the screen that we can't see your face (especially a problem in large room videoconferencing).

It is just as important that you notice the other person's body language. Try to speak at their pace and match their demeanour. This is called 'mirroring'. You don't do it slavishly – that would be creepy. But many psychological studies underline its effectiveness in building rapport and forging connections. Syncing up with someone's body language – picking up on their 'vibe' – can send positive and non-conflicting signals, which build rapport.

AUDITORY

The way you speak – the tone and timbre of your voice – provides immediate clues about your confidence level. A thin, strained voice can come across as tentative and make you sound like prey. On the other hand, a diaphragm-deep voice emanates self-assuredness and communicates strength. It's also worth noting that speech patterns, such as rapid pacing, rising intonations or repetitive uses of the same phrase, irritate the listener and detract from the importance of the point being made. This is not the ideal impression to leave people with when you're aiming to be clear, professional and reassuringly calm.

There are two common problems people have with the voice:

Problem
Speaking too quietly.

Remedy
Increase the physical distance between you and the listener or, when you are presenting from the stage, speak to the people on the back row, furthest away from you. You will be forced to project your voice – or your audience will shout 'speak up!'.

Problem
Speaking too fast.

Remedy
Pause before you start speaking. Think of traffic lights.

Red. Yellow. Green.

Stop. Get ready. Go.

Take a breath. Make eye contact with your audience. Speak. At various points maybe ask a question (rhetorical or otherwise) to punctuate the word flow, re-engage the audience and give yourself a breather.

Stress influences voice quality. When you're tense, especially in a hunched posture, your throat and vocal cords tighten, making your voice sound shaky, constrained and weak. This is why dedicating time to cultivating your voice and speech patterns is crucial: consider voice exercises or breathing and relaxation techniques. You can find plenty of these exercises online.

If you do nothing else, do this

There is one exercise you *must* do just before you go online to speak or are about to deliver your bit of a presentation. You need to warm up your mouth and lips ready for action. We mouth the phrase 'I want to kick you!' three times – and we really move the mouth muscles to get everything working.

We use this phrase because it moves your mouth in all the directions you'll need to employ when speaking. Try saying it now. Slowly. Articulate every sound precisely and open your mouth wide: 'I – want – to – kick – you!'

See? Allied to some sort of physical movement – such as an arm and leg shake or a dynamic movement to get the blood flowing – it will get you gunned up and ready to perform.

If you worry about being overheard or seen when you are warming up, just take yourself off to a quiet corner out on the stairwell or to the restroom or just mouth *'I want to kick you!'* behind your hand. But *do* it.

Doing so will make a massive difference to the way you are perceived when you open your mouth.

SEMANTIC

The words you use are important. Your body language and voice actually enhance the impact of your words manifold. As for the words themselves, use *fewer and simpler* words rather than more words and more complicated words.

Remember some useful tips:

– No one remembers numbers. Everyone remembers stories.

Including stories about numbers.

– Words have context. The context is often in the head of the listener. Think not just about the words you want to use but also about the context of those words – how they will be *received*. Clients don't want to hear gloom and doom if they are already in a difficult situation. Nor are they likely to react well to you making light of a serious situation.

– Do not use jargon words that do not create pictures in people's heads.

– Keep it simple. Say 'win' instead of 'realise your potential'; say 'sell your company' instead of 'arrive at a liquidity event'.

– Prioritise your messages: have no more than three messages you want your audience to remember.

ENERGY

When you add all of these things up, there's an intangible quality at play: the energy you project. When we refer to energy, we're not talking about anything mystical or esoteric. It revolves around your genuine intentions and demeanour – qualities that people can instantly sense. Specifically, this involves:

– a heartfelt desire to *help* your clients
– a genuine belief in your product or service

These are the hallmarks of a great salesperson and of top-performing sales teams.

Faith in your product or service ties directly to this desire to help. It's implicit that this belief isn't just superficial – it implies a thorough understanding of your product, its strengths and weaknesses, an awareness of competitors and their offering, and a comprehensive knowledge of the industry. Simply put, your conviction should be grounded in reality, not just unbridled enthusiasm. We cover this in more depth in week three. But, as a rule, the more convinced you are about your product or service's ability to help a client, the more persuasive you will be. *People buy conviction.*

Tenacity is something you will need to cultivate – it's the drive that propels you forward, ensuring eventual success. The gestation period for a sale in our world of consulting can be eighteen months from initial contact to actual delivery. And there are many hurdles to overcome in the intervening period:

– getting hold of all the right people if the decision involves multiple stakeholders
– sending proposals and revising them multiple times as new information affects the configuration of a project
– events which derail the process (economic recessions, corporate blocks on expenditure towards the year end, pandemics, etc)
– delays, obfuscation, new circumstances. All get in the way.

You will need to stay the course. It will be frustrating, but you will get there eventually if you remain positive, friendly and resourceful. Be the partner who keeps focus and deals with whatever is thrown at you. That, in its own right, says a lot about you and signals to your client that you aren't just a fair-weather friend. You're serious about partnership.

THE VALUE OF YOUR PERSONAL BRAND IN SALES

People don't only buy your product or service. They also invest in the person from whom they are buying. They buy *you.* And they usually buy from people they like. That's human nature.

That doesn't mean that being successful in sales is about being attractive, gregarious or kind. It's much more than that. It's about being skilful in many aspects of the sales process: preparation, holding structured sales conversations, following up, networking, emotional intelligence, listening ability, observation skills and long-term relationship building. We will deep dive into all of these skills in the next four weeks of our programme.

Creating your personal brand is not about changing yourself. It's about being *aware* of yourself and consciously pulling together all the skills, attitudes and personality traits that you already have into a unique brand. Because that brand is authentic to you, because it's based exclusively on the work you've done this week, it will help you feel confident and genuine when you are selling.

SUMMARY

Our first week together is done. We've thrown a lot at you but by now you should have a rock-solid foundation on which to build the skills we cover in the next four weeks. If we've laboured the point that you need to get your head straight about your attitude towards selling, and that your beliefs about it and about yourself are the cornerstones of being an effective salesperson, it's because we want – above everything – you to be you. Your selling style must reflect the sort of person you are; that way, it'll feel right because it will come naturally to you.

This week we've focused on you. In week two, we're turning 180 degrees to focus on *them* – your clients.

Week Two:
The client

'Make a customer, not a sale'
KATHERINE BARCHETTI

You always sell to people

Whether you're a business leader, the parent of a teenager or a salesperson, you would probably agree that it's impossible to force someone to do something. The strategy of coercion simply doesn't work and often has negative consequences. The only way to influence someone's behaviour is to engage with them, so that they act in their own best interest and of their own free will. Which is why we always aim to create partnership with our clients. Partnership is based on trust and must be mutually beneficial. And as you can only be in charge of your side of it, let's focus on what you need to do.

First of all, let's remind ourselves that clients are people too. We all know it and yet it is amazing how many times you ask business people 'Tell me about your clients' and you hear in response 'They are companies with $50m EBITDA', or 'government departments', or 'consumer packaged-goods companies'. All too often we describe our clients as entities – companies, brands or structures.

And when describing ourselves, our CVs, résumés, reports and social posts are full of the same, impersonal language: 'I work for Unilever', 'our Microsoft client' and 'this department's priorities', for example. We constantly make statements which ignore the human side of business.

So let's begin week two with one simple truth – you do not sell to Unilever, Microsoft, banks, conglomerates, management consultancies or retailers. You do not sell to commercial structures. You can only ever sell to people.

It is true that people can be influenced by the companies they work for; but they still remain people, individuals. Clients also have their own personalities and preferred behavioural styles. If we want to communicate with them successfully and build good and long-lasting relationships we need to understand them as people.

Understanding your client's personality

A great salesperson is like a great detective.

The $64m question: how do you spot which type your client is without getting them to answer the personality questionnaire? A great salesperson is like a great detective: you look and listen out for clues. Get enough clues and you'll be able to work out your client's dominant behavioural style (or combination of styles). Here are the clues you need to notice:

How they greet you

Are they friendly? Do they offer you a drink, make small talk (*Amiable or Expressive*)? Do they act professionally, straight to business, no niceties? (*Analytical or Driver*).

How they dress

Formal, immaculate appearance (*Driver – think Sheryl Sandberg*). Scruffy, look like they got dressed in the dark and exhibit the attitude that clothes are functional (*Analytical – think Mark Zuckerberg*). Have their own style, maybe flamboyant (*Expressive – think Boris Johnson*). Anonymous (*Amiable – think a typical civil servant*).

Level of eye contact (online and offline)

Little eye contact, maybe reading off or looking at another screen to the side of the camera (*Analytical or Amiable*). Direct eye contact (*Driver or Expressive*).

The way they speak or answer questions

Short, clipped language; simple yes/no answers with no accompanying explanation, use of the word 'I' (*Driver*). Long, complicated answers with lots of qualification and explanation of the thinking behind them; asking you detailed questions (*Analytical*). Verbose and lacking logical flow but loud and with humour (*Expressive*). Use of the words 'we' and 'us'; courteous, supportive body language; smiling when you are speaking, looking like they are listening to you and enjoying it (*Amiable*).

Their LinkedIn profile

No profile, personal picture and 'About' section; standard backdrop template; scant information and few – perhaps even no – posts (*Analytical – they think LinkedIn is a waste of time and just for people who want a job*).

Lots of professional qualifications, MBA brags and work accomplishments strung together in bullet points of polysyllabic words chosen to make their work seem important and complicated. Personal picture but standard backdrop template (*Driver*).

High-quality picture of the person; personalised backdrop picture of, for example, them on a stage with other important people, with the branding of the high-profile conference on display in the background; loquacious 'About' section, setting forth their philosophy of life and vision for the business they work in, which is entertaining to read and scattered with personal stories. Up-to-date recommendations from clients and colleagues (*Expressive – they care about their image, so they lavish more care and attention on their Linkedin profile than any other group*).

Nice personal picture, against a backdrop of the person in a group photo with their team or family. Personal information and lots of mentions of their team members whom they praise and credit with their own success. They share a lot online, comment on and applaud the achievements of their company and colleagues (*Amiable*).

SETTING: ONLINE

Analyticals want to remain at a distance and objective. They may present a blurred-out background so you can't see anything behind them, or they are off camera altogether. They do not like showing personality or personal space – it's private. What they need to understand is that the other groups, especially those focused on relationships (Expressives and Amiables), wonder what they are hiding and don't like talking to a blank screen. Analyticals often use several screens (to have precise information at hand), so lots of Analyticals do not look at the camera. They look at the important things *for them* (facts, charts, etc) rather than at the people on the call, which are the important things for everyone else.

The background has been carefully choreographed (bookshelves, guitars on the wall, etc) to convey personality and project an image (*Expressive*). They are well lit on screen. They will also smile, nod and move a lot. Expressives like being on TV and to show off their 'set'.

A plain background devoid of any colour or distractions (*Driver*). Drivers often use a corporate screen behind them, conveying they are strictly business, or something simple and functional. They do not move much in front of the camera and are just a 'talking head'.

Natural setting, at home, badly lit, a bit chaotic (*Amiable*). Not much thought has gone into it. Happy to let you into their home, warts and all – a cat walking on the table in front of the camera, the dog barking. They are likely to have a cosy mug in their hands.

SETTING: OFFLINE

Lots of family photos (also on their laptop and phone), personal memorabilia – personalised mugs, plants, toys, something to do with their hobbies, children and pets – on their desk. You will be offered biscuits, small talk, simple welcoming courtesies and comfy soft furnishings (*Amiables*).

A plain desk with nothing on it, certificates of accomplishment and professional qualification on the wall, minimalist, no offer of a drink but straight to business. The Driver does not care about your agenda because there is only one agenda – theirs. They care about control and are more likely to have a clock (to control time) and a phone (to control everyone) than charts or presentation decks (they don't need them).

Colour, interesting pictures on the wall, affable handshake, visually stimulating environment, lots of talking, post-it notes, magazines (*Expressive*). A workspace is a place of stimulation for Expressives. They decorate it to project personality, to show off their prowess and to impress you.

Physical distance between you and them, probably a table or a desk, documents shared and read through line by line, no social niceties, long meetings to discuss details with an agenda (*Analytical*).

We sell to people, not organisations. But your clients work in companies which also exhibit dominant behavioural styles – just like people. Do you think a sales presentation to Lenovo would be exactly the same as one to Apple? No, it wouldn't. Apple values design, simplicity, innovation and aesthetics – all traits which come from its Expressive-Driver founder, Steve Jobs. Lenovo speaks a different language: functionality and discounted price. Driver, Analytical. Just look at the two companies' websites – they tell you all you need to know about the behavioural style that's valued in the organisation.

You know who you're selling to – now what?

The four pillars of selling

Once you've pieced together the clues and know who you are selling to, you have to start thinking about what you can do for them. There are four things you can do for them. These are the four pillars of successful sales.

- Enhance
- Enlighten
- Engage
- Exceed

We will cover each pillar separately, although it's important to remember that you cannot use only one or two of them; they work as a whole, not separately.

ENHANCE

The first and most important pillar of sales is to *enhance* the life and/or the business of your client. Selling is all about helping a client to effect change. Change in fortune or circumstances, change in momentum or direction, change in effectiveness or efficiency, change in the results they are achieving. So your main task is to reveal to the client all the wonderful changes that will happen in their business and their life, thanks to you and your product or service. Conversely, you may need to help them understand what will happen if they *don't* make the necessary changes by using you and your service or product. Either way, you are painting them a picture of the future – the situation *before* your intervention and how it improves *after* your involvement.

What are you selling?
(i) Your value proposition

First of all, it's essential to be able to articulate in simple words how you can help your clients and how you can change their lives for the better. You need to be able to explain a specific benefit to your clients' business: to increase revenues, decrease their costs or improve their efficiency. Effective salespeople sell increased productivity, more effective customer service, less downtime on production lines, lower costs, quicker response times, higher return on investment. Ineffective salespeople sell *features* rather than benefits: widgets, legal services, office space, factory equipment, computer systems.

'Effective salespeople sell results. Ineffective salespeople sell things'

What is it that you actually sell?

Write down exactly how you enhance the life of your client and the performance of their business. Include why you are different and better than your competitors. This is called your *value proposition*.

_____

_____

_____

Write down what problems you help them to solve.

_____

_____

_____

What problems can they avoid, thanks to your product/services?

_____

_____

_____

If you write down something like 'We sell equipment for regulating the temperature in the OTC production plant', you're trying to sell features and you need to go further to reveal all the *benefits* of working with you (and not with your competitor) – today, tomorrow and the day after.

You should also avoid vague, generic statements such as 'my client will grow their business with me'. Be precise – by how much will their business grow? Use numbers to substantiate your claim. Include past examples of effect with other clients, independent audits of the results you have produced or aggregate growth in revenues achieved. If you don't have such proofs, find them.

If you have a team, it's vital that you all share a consistent articulation of what value you bring to clients. Test what members of your team say now. Ask three people in your team to tell you exactly how they improve clients' lives with your product or service. And how they describe the benefit to the client of working with you. There's a big chance you'll find inconsistency in what you hear. If you do, agree on a description of how your team adds value to your clients' businesses and ensure that everyone understands it and uses it.

(ii) Consistent communication

The second point is to make sure that your value proposition is consistent across all your client and industry communication: on your website, in sales collateral, during conference presentations and partner events, when pitching and networking. If you can, help your clients to use this same language when they talk about your firm with their own colleagues.

For example, we describe what we do for clients using a metaphor. We say:

'Formula 1 pit crews change the tyres, refuel the car, service the engine and wipe the driver's visor in just 1.8 seconds to get the car back on the racetrack performing at its best. We reset our clients' sales teams fast and send them back out into the world able to perform more effectively so they win more, more often.'

It gives clients an easy way to explain how we help them, which also, by association with F1, conveys our elite effectiveness.

It is as important to ensure your personal brand communication syncs with your own value proposition as it is to make sure your company's value proposition is clear, differentiated and easy for clients to understand and explain.

Does your LinkedIn profile, especially the 'About' section, explain clearly and precisely how you add value at work or to your clients? Does it say what you do simply and in an engaging and interesting way? Most people pay little or no attention to their LinkedIn profile. They only pay attention to it when they are looking for a new job. Too late! Your personal brand needs as much attention as your company value proposition. Why? Where's the first place potential clients will go to check you out? LinkedIn. If they are greeted with a low-quality picture of you (or, even worse, no picture at all), a word-vomit of polysyllabic words and a handful of out-of-date testimonials, it's not a great first impression, is it?

Speaking of first impressions. When you do meet, make the

momentum. Too many salespeople start out being servile – wanting to please their client above all else. They become afraid to say what they believe lest they anger their client. But you cannot give good advice from a 'bended knee' position. You cannot enhance a client's world if you live in perpetual fear of pissing people off. There is a saying in sales that 'you get the clients you deserve'. If you allow yourself to be bullied by being a pleaser rather than an advisor, your clients won't respect you, your company or the advice you proffer.

Make the momentum by setting expectations at the start of your relationship. State and show what it is like to work with you. Let's show you what this looks like.

Andrea was a colleague of ours. She changed companies many times, but her long-standing client, P&G, always followed her wherever she went. For thirty years she was P&G's 'go-to' guy in the field of communications strategy. We asked her the secret of this phenomenal client loyalty. She distilled her approach down to three basic principles:

1. I always act in the interests of my clients' business or brand first.
2. I always act in the interests of my company second.
3. I always act in the interests of my client and myself third.

Everywhere she went and whichever part of P&G's portfolio of brands she worked on, she always stated these principles in her first meeting with any new clients. That way, she established how she would always operate with them and she set their expectations. So they always had a consistent experience and, even if it made her irritating to some clients in the short term (because she wouldn't always do their bidding), it gained her huge credibility. They knew that not only did she understand their business, but that they could always expect her to speak and act conscientiously – even if that was to the detriment of her and her employer's financial interests.

For Andrea, that sometimes means that she has to advise her client *not* to buy something from her. Yes, you read that right: not to buy. Why? Because in this particular circumstance, her product will not be the most effective investment *at the moment*. Such honesty is valuable – it shows sincere and honest ambition to act in the best interests of your client. Losing a sale in the short term builds trus, and trust builds long-lasting relationships. Long-lasting relationships make both parties wealthy. (Andrea may lose the odd sale but she and her company are doing all right.)

Finally, how do you use your direct day-to-day communication with clients to enhance their lives? Emails, phone calls, reports, status updates, Slack channel messages and loads of other written and verbal channels are how clients experience you and your brand every day. There is a right way to communicate day to day. And the wrong way.

Read this email and imagine you're the client.

> Hi Guillaume,
>
> How are you? Hope all is well. We observe that our recommendations to run the additional performance marketing campaigns on our platform were not implemented. This makes a $500K gap in your spend vs the spend I recommended you make earlier in the year.
>
> Last month, during our phone call, you agreed to start the additional campaigns within a week. But today we are almost at the end of Q3 and they have not started, which is not in line with the initially agreed investment flow.
>
> I acknowledge that you have had changes in the team and some business problems in the middle of the year. I hope that you will fix all the issues soon, so that we can work efficiently in our partnership going forward. Will you be adding people to your team temporarily to launch the campaigns on our platform? It is really important to catch

up with the investment flow on your side and to implement our recommendations.

Happy to jump on a call in case you have any questions,

Thanks for your collaboration in this important partnership matter.

Kind Regards,

Franck

How would it make you feel if you were Guillaume? The tone of voice is supercilious – Franck sounds like a schoolteacher telling off a naughty child. (Who's the client here? Him or, er, the client?) It reeks of self-interest. You can tell that Franck is panicking – he can see his sales bonus disappearing over the horizon. His tone of voice is patronising: Franck tells the client he needs to 'catch up' and pretty much accuses the client of lying and failing to honour their commitment.

Here's the right way.

Hi Guillaume,

I hope you enjoyed our business breakfast seminar on AI last week. I'm attaching the report we produced on the back of it which includes a brief synopsis of the five key takeaways. I have expanded on one area in particular, which shows great potential to increase your retailer network's sales conversion ratios. Once you've read it, let's fix a time to discuss that potential more precisely.

Whilst I have you, I noticed that the performance marketing campaign scheduled for Q3 is not yet under way. Do let me know if you are encountering issues with getting it under way. It occurred to me that you have added three new people to your team this quarter and it will take time to bed them in. Would it be helpful if:

(i) We run weekly sessions for each new member of your team over the next month to familiarise them with the performance marketing tools?

> *(ii) We send two members of our team into your offices for seven days at the end of this month to help you manage the scale up for the Q3 programme?*
>
> *If there is anything we can do to help you and to get these new campaigns under way, we are ready, willing and able! Shall we jump on a call to see what might work best? I am available tomorrow morning or the following afternoon. Let me know which you prefer or send me a calendar invitation for when suits you best and I will accommodate.*
>
> *In the meantime, very best wishes and I hope you find the AI synopsis attached thought-provoking.*
>
> *Franck*

This response sets a collaborative tone, not a scolding one. It took us time to craft because it should take time to craft a thoughtful response to a sensitive issue. Franck's original attempt was obviously dashed off in the heat of the moment. It was written in anger with only a cursory pretence at politeness. It employed threats and accusations and placed the entire emphasis on the client to solve the issue.

Our more subtle response is much more ameliorative. It seeks not just to keep the relationship intact but to *enhance* our partnership. We show we are in this together, that we empathise with the client's situation and are able to help. We raise the problematic issue only *after* we have first taken care of our relationship; firstly, by adding new value (the report on the AI seminar); and, secondly, with the offer of even more value to come (a new product). Finally, we make it feel as if the problem is due to either an oversight or a capacity issue – no blame is attached to it; instead, all the focus is on moving towards a resolution. The sign-off steers the client towards a timeline for taking action but gives him options. It does not present the client with *faux* concern or a coded ultimatum.

When the day-to-day experience of working with you is

consistent with the value proposition you promise, it is easier for clients to feel the enhancement you bring to their work life. And if they feel that, they will want you to enhance their work life in other areas as well. Which means more sales.

ENLIGHTEN

One of the most profound ways you can add value to your clients is to stretch their vision of their own business and expand their horizons. This is all about encouraging thought beyond conventional boundaries, revealing new insights and ideas and presenting a fresh vision for the future of their business.

For most companies offering products or services, their clients are constantly torn between having to deal with what the present throws at them (dealing with inflation, retaining and attracting talent, driving operational efficiencies) and becoming future-fit for a rapidly changing world (AI, escalating energy prices, climate change and geo-political instability). In PwC's 2023 global survey of 4,410 CEOs, the message from these business leaders was 'evolve or die'; yet 40 per cent of CEOs don't think their company will be viable in a decade from today if they continue on their current path. Why? Because they aren't spending enough time reinventing their business for the future.

> *'Change is the law of life. And those who look only to the past or present are certain to miss the future'*
> JOHN F. KENNEDY

When we ask business leadership teams how they spend their time, on average they say they spend 60 per cent focused on the now (they think it should be 50 per cent); they spend 30 per cent on the near-term future (they think that should be 20 per cent). And they only spend 10 per cent of their time focused on the long-term future (they think it should be 30 per cent). Too many clients are so immersed in the day-to-day, in sorting out the urgent, that they simply don't have the time to focus on the important (the future). Consequently, companies often miss the future. Kodak, Nokia, Blockbuster, Debenhams – it's already a big graveyard and AI is going to add to the body count.

All of which tells us that if you anticipate the future – those important issues that will be coming over the horizon towards your client – and you come with solutions to those issues, you will be welcomed with open arms. Because they don't have the time to do it themselves.

It's crucial to keep up with all the news, trends and patterns in your business universe. Look at the general landscape and overlay your client's specific business perspective – this can often be a catalyst for identifying previously unseen angles, opportunities and threats.

Your aim is to inspire your clients with new ideas and solutions. Show them what's going on in other industries or markets. Brainstorm with them. Facilitate workshops for them on trends and new technologies. Invite them to new product demos and breakfast briefings on topics relevant to their universe. Demonstrate genuine interest, with no agenda other than to *help* them.

Helping your client navigate the future makes you a very valuable strategic partner – one worth listening to.

Success story

What does this look like in practice? A collaboration between L'Oréal and Google led to the creation of a successful beauty product. Google invests heavily in the relationships they have with their biggest clients by sharing with them interesting trends and insights into consumer behaviour. Google does this at no additional cost, because they see such help as part of their enduring collaboration.

In the case of L'Oréal, Google did a deep dive into consumer behaviour across the entire beauty industry. Research spotted a growing interest among women in a specific style of hair colouring called ombré. This trend, initially adopted by celebrities and fashion models, quickly captivated the public. Yet, as ombré colouring was exclusive to professional beauty salons, achieving this sought-after look was beyond the reach of most people. Seizing this opportunity, L'Oréal launched a do-it-yourself home ombré colouring kit, which immediately flew off the shelves and created a brand-new revenue stream with dramatic sales results.

Shedding new light on the consumer or business environment doesn't only help unlock potential for product development, it can also help clients spot problems. So don't underestimate your own knowledge and observation. Even if you do not have huge resources that you can dedicate to the analysis of your client's business, sharing your own awareness of trends, observations and ideas will demonstrate your sincere interest in their business. Read a couple of articles, listen to a podcast, search for recent interviews – do the homework every journalist does before talking to someone they are going to interview themselves. You will see how much easier the conversation will flow – and how much more productive it is for both of you. It is a far superior model to generate sales than waiting for your client to send you a brief.

ENGAGE

Business is about the value you bring but it is also about the connection you manage to forge with your clients. Your clients choose to work with you and your team as individuals, and it's you and your team that they will recommend if they enjoy the working relationship. But in this era of information overload, abundant networking opportunities and an overwhelming array of companies eager to offer their services, your clients' attention can easily get distracted by competitors. Therefore, being 'engaging' is an evolutionary necessity.

The truth is that human beings are selling all the time. Our point of view about an issue, a recommendation of a movie or restaurant, to go to the gym or have a night in with a tub of ice cream – these are all sales conversations because we are often seeking to enthuse, to persuade, to warn or to recruit to a cause. And, for most people, most of the time, it all feels very natural. We use colloquial speech, our bodies are animated, we smile, frown, express emotion and rattle off myriad reasons why this or that is the best course of action or the solution to any situation. We are natural salespeople, natural communicators, natural persuaders and enthusiasts. We are naturally engaging.

But something happens to us when we are at work. We go all 'professional'. We get stiff and formal. We think we have to curtail all that enthusiasm and, instead of being creative and telling an interesting narrative, we churn out endless PowerPoint charts with endless lists of data and facts to support our case, all presented in a dull monotone. We are the opposite of engaging. We lose our audience's attention and lose the sales opportunity as a result.

Getting and keeping the client's attention

Getting and keeping people's attention was codified by the great philosopher Aristotle three thousand years ago. Aristotle identified three core elements of persuasive engagement:

Ethos: the character of the person and their credentials on the issue or subject
Logos: the logic of their argument, facts and figures
Pathos: use of emotion and connection to 'move' an audience.

Back then, these were subjects of serious study for anyone keen to carve out a reputation as a lawyer, politician or advocate. And these principles still hold today.

Probably the most famous manifestations of modern-day engagement are TED Talks. World experts on pretty much every subject under the sun keep audiences in the auditorium and online spellbound for eighteen minutes and attract audience numbers by the million for each talk. The academic Carmine Gallo made a study of the top five hundred most-watched TED Talks and discovered that, on average, they were split 10 per cent ethos, 25 per cent logos and a whopping 65 per cent pathos. What does this tell us? That the best communication in the world is primarily made up of stories.

If you look at most sales presentations or documents, the ratio is the other way around. Heavy on statistics, facts, numbers, bullet points, graphs, pie charts, bell curves and spreadsheets, but devoid of human-interest stories, dry as dust and way too long.

Writing and presenting that engages

Your opening needs to arrest the clients' attention. To do this, your words need to trigger the release of cortisol. Cortisol is best known as the stress hormone, though it is also the excitement hormone. Produced in response to stressful situations, it is central to the 'fight or flight' response. When your cortisol levels are high, you may experience sweating, anxiety and a desire to either fight or run away. In business, you trigger it by alerting the client to a clear and present danger that needs addressing: a steep fall in profits, a calamitous decline in sales revenue, a disruptive technology which poses an existential threat to a company's survival.

To engage with anyone, you need to get their undivided attention from the start. If you don't get their undivided attention, you won't sell anything. So grab your client's attention with an opening statement that stops them in their tracks and makes them want to read or listen on. Most sales presentations start with a regurgitation of the client's brief or some craven platitudes thanking the client for the opportunity to pitch. These send the client to sleep. Don't waste the opportunity to make the momentum: think like a TV presenter or a bestselling author – trigger the readers' curiosity with an opening that grabs them by the eyeballs.

Next, you need to trigger **dopamine.** Dopamine is the hormone responsible for many addictions, including the common addiction to your phone, because it gives a 'hit' of pleasure. In business, dopamine rewards us with feelings of pleasure when we follow an argument and stay focused. You trigger it by using a few facts judiciously, by having a golden thread of logic that's easy to follow and makes it easy for the reader to navigate your presentation. Again, too many sales presentations are far too detailed and drown the reader in a sea of statistics. People don't remember facts, they remember stories – fact![1]

Use only the killer stats and make the effort to weave them into a simple narrative.

Finally, the wonder drug of persuasion: **oxytocin**. This is what helps humans identify with each other. Oxytocin is sometimes called the 'relationship hormone' because it's responsible for feelings of closeness and warmth. It is triggered when we do a nice thing for someone else, when we feel trust and when we show our vulnerability.

In a buying environment, oxytocin is the hormone you trigger in your clients when you take them out to dinner, meet them on the golf course, or send them a book you think they'll enjoy. A client experiencing high levels of oxytocin is less likely to be risk-averse, and more likely to be open to change.

Oxytocin is the reason that warm relationships are so important in complex B2B sales. Taking time to invest in relationships with your clients pays dividends because it taps into how humans' hormones have evolved to ensure our species' survival.

One of the ways to trigger oxytocin is by associating you and your service in your client's mind with people and services that they already trust. It works because the mind is always looking for shortcuts that help it decide to do or not do something. And one of the shortest cuts is to transfer the feelings of trust from one person to another.

For example, you're probably familiar with the little notices in hotel bathrooms which ask you to reuse your bath towels. Hotels ask

---

[1] *Stories, Statistics and Memory*, Thomas Graeber, assistant professor of business administration at Harvard Business School.

you to do this because it saves them huge laundry bills – though they dress it up as being for the sake of the environment. They save money, you feel virtuous – everyone wins. Except the generic notice isn't that effective at getting hotel guests to comply in big numbers. So various hotel groups have experimented with different wording for the little cards they place in bathrooms and used researchers to measure the results. They discovered that one particular wording format works more effectively than others.

Researchers tried two different wording formats: the first told guests that *previous guests who had stayed in the same room they were now staying in* had re-used their towels more than once. The second format told guests that previous guests who had stayed in the *same hotel* they were currently staying in had re-used their towels more than once.

'We found that guests cut their towel use significantly when told of the behaviour of *previous guests in their room,*' said the lead researcher Dr Gerhard Reese. With the 'staying in the same room' scenario, guests used, on average, one towel per person per day. This compared with 1.6 towels per person per day for those told of behaviour in the hotel as a whole. This amounted to a 40 per cent saving in the number of towels needing to be washed.

These results are consistent with a handful of similar studies conducted in the USA. 'Humans are social beings,' explained Dr Reese. 'People want to be accepted into groups and so we act in ways that make us belong. Instinctively, we feel close to those who have used a hotel room before us, believing that they are similar to ourselves. Thus we are more likely to follow their behaviour.'[2]

---

[2] From a study by Dr Gerhard Reese of the Université du Luxembourg published in Science Daily, March 2014.
https://www.sciencedaily.com/releases/2014/03/140324104426.htm.

When you put all this together you get a sales presentation that goes something like this:

ATTENTION (trigger cortisol by using logos)
Smartphones have left people with such short attention spans that a goldfish can hold a thought for longer. In 2020, the average human's attention span was twelve seconds. Just two years later it had fallen by a huge 33 per cent.

BENEFIT (trigger dopamine by using pathos)
We're going to give you a technique that can grab your audience's attention for longer than the average human's eight-second attention span (goldfish have an attention span of nine seconds), which has made millions of people's pitches more persuasive.

CREDENTIALS (trigger oxytocin by using ethos)
We've been helping salespeople improve their communications impact for over two decades, working with some of the world's most dynamic organisations.

DIRECTION (cortisol again – the need for action)

Use pictures, very few words and only the most essential numbers. For example:

2020 – 12 secs   2022 – 8 secs   Fish – 9 secs

Now, try it out for yourself on one of your own presentations.

A well-crafted pitch stimulates questions and discussion; it creates dialogue. If you've engaged your audience, you will get client commentary and dialogue. Dialogue builds relationships so be receptive to client questions and viewpoints – it will often be insightful.

If you lecture people, mistake complexity for brilliance, bombard them with statistics and miss the cultural clues, you'll leave empty-handed. We know the CEO of a big telecom company who admitted that if she didn't understand what was being pitched to her by an advisory firm, she didn't seek clarification or bother to ask questions. She just didn't appoint them. Her reasoning was: 'If you don't have clarity at the initial pitch stage and you can't communicate your ideas simply, what will it be like to collaborate with you in the long term?'

> 'The ability to simplify means to eliminate the unnecessary
> so that the necessary may speak'
> HANS HOFMANN

EXCEED

Exceeding a client's expectations isn't just about providing excellent service or an exceptional product; it's also about offering that added (little) extra.

The rationale for doing this is straightforward: exceeding expectations helps build your reputation with your clients and in the market as *different* and *better*. This ensures your existing clients keep choosing you time after time and new clients want to meet you.

In sales, going the extra mile requires added effort, but consider it a long-term deposit in the bank of client trust and loyalty. Whether you're designing a custom dashboard for project data access, offering extended post-launch support, delivering the project ahead of schedule, or granting them exclusive beta-access to your latest products – each of these gestures serves as a memorable value add for your client. Such thoughtful touches solidify your relationship and insulate you from competitive incursion.

One thing to watch out for: in your mission to exceed expectations, don't do damage to yourself or your team and don't be obsequious. For example, here's a story shared by our client, Jessica, based in Bangkok.

Jessica had a supplier from London. Aiming to provide excellent client service, the supplier would call Jessica daily at 9am (Jessica's local time) to update her on their project's progress. Given her busy schedule, the supplier believed he had found the perfect time to catch Jessica before her day got hectic. However, Jessica realised that these calls were being made at 3am London time. Rather than feeling well served, she felt uncomfortable and guilty about his sacrifice. She told him that an email update would suffice. The supplier's intention was to go the extra mile; instead, he went a step too far and made his client feel awkward.

Whilst exceeding expectations in your professional capacity is useful, it is in the personal domain that it can be really effective. It's not just about helping improve the performance of your client's company. It's also about helping your client personally. To look good. To learn. To share their expertise. To make them feel valued.

Create opportunities to do things of mutual benefit and which enhance your client's reputation in their industry, in your industry, in the business universe and in the media.

– Speak at each other's company conferences
– Invite them to speak to your firm about their business
– Invite their colleagues or kids to a product demonstration or

special workshop. If you're in tech, run a session for parents of teens on gaming culture to help them understand their children's world. Invite your client to speak at it and bring their kids
– Offer your expertise to share at your clients' 'lunch and learn' sessions to help their colleagues get a glimpse into how you help them and how your industry works
– Invite your client to an internal training session. For example, we ask clients to write a brief for our trainees to work on and then come judge the results. The client gets free ideas, and the trainees hear the perspective of a client on the subject of the training.

How to incorporate the four pillars of success in your selling?

This week, reflect on how you can incorporate the four pillars into your strategic and tactical interactions with clients. Create a list of initiatives that you can suggest for specific client groups or for each client individually. It's crucial that both you and your team have a clear understanding of the expected outcomes for each initiative.

Client/industry initiative: _____

_____

_____

_____

Now, let's break down what you can do for each 'E' of the four pillars of sales.

For example:
Enhance:
Create your value proposition, for you personally as a brand and for your company/product/service to show how you add value uniquely.

You: _____

_____

_____

Company/product/service: _____
_____
_____

Enlighten:

Prepare an overview of competitors, industry issues and trends for one specific client. This will set the stage for discussions on the upcoming year's strategy.

Engage:

Turn one of your sales presentations into a brief story which uses ethos, logos and pathos. Make sure the start will trigger cortisol, the logical reasoning and/or numbers trigger dopamine, and the story triggers oxytocin by demonstrating that you have produced excellent results for clients just like the new one you want to help.

Exceed:

Start creating a 'Peoplebase' of useful information about your clients – hobbies, interests, significant dates, names of children and partner, subjects they are particularly interested in, etc – so that you move beyond a purely functional relationship.

SUMMARY

Always remember that you are selling to people, not to institutions or companies. Like you, people are individuals, with foibles, passions, prejudices, opinions and their own unique personalities. The more you know about the person or people you are selling to, the more you can help them. Use the four Es as pillars on which to build your relationship with your clients. Show how you *enhance* the results they can achieve; *enlighten* them with insights that stretch their vision of what *can* be achieved; *engage* with them in a way that inspires, informs, educates and entertains them; and *exceed* their expectations so you're dealing with them as human beings rather than as a mere route to revenue.

Week Three:
Science – the rational side of selling

'Everybody's typing. Who's thinking?'
CLIENT BEING SHOWN AROUND AN OPEN-PLAN OFFICE WITH
THREE HUNDRED PEOPLE ALL SITTING AT COMPUTERS

This week our focus will be on the rational side of your sales approach – the science of selling. We'll be focused on:

- your expertise on your own and your client's business
- what questions you should ask to identify new opportunities and challenges for your clients
- how to package your thinking
- structuring the sales conversation
- what techniques work best to handle objections
- closing the sale.

That's a lot of work. And all of it takes time. So let's start with what to do in order to create time to think (rather than merely react).

DEEP WORK – MAKING THE TIME TO BE BRILLIANT
'I haven't got the time', we hear you say. Yes you do. Most of us work almost exclusively at the 'surface' level – skimming along the surface reacting to things: email, voicemail, endless 'to do' lists, social media. We live in a world of digital distraction, where we skip from one urgent task to another. Great salespeople don't do that; they deliberately carve out 'deep work' time. They turn off all alerts and other distractions.

They go to a quiet place and refuse to let other people or tasks distract them. And in that space, they do something very old-fashioned: they concentrate on one thing that is important. Not urgent, *important*.

In today's hybrid working world, it's possible to find a space where deep work can be done. Part of the discipline of deep work is identifying somewhere that you mentally and physically associate with thinking or working on bigger issues than merely task response. Find that space. Go to it physically when deep work is what you need to do. And make it habitual. Start with 40 minutes a day. Think that's impossible? Ask yourself: is it really impossible or am I being a 'busy fool'? Chasing your tail, running around, reacting.

Could you free up 5 per cent of your week for deep work? In the average forty-hour working week, that's two hours a week. Imagine: two hours just to think. In a month, that'll be eight hours – a whole extra working day. Imagine what that will do for your selling effectiveness. And if you can get your team to do deep work in a similar way, you will multiply their cumulative effectiveness many times over.

PUTTING DEEP WORK TO USE

There are two areas to master in the rational side of selling:

1. Your business environment: A comprehensive understanding of your product or service, competitors' products, industry trends and overall market dynamics.

2. Your client's business: Really get to grips with their product, operations, competitors, industry and how they make money.

Ordinary salespeople usually try to master the first one. They become subject area experts. Those who master both areas are *super* salespeople. They become *trusted advisors* to their clients. You want to be the latter. Trusted advisors are strategically vital to their clients. They move beyond mere vendor or supplier status. They are listened to and counsel their clients at the highest levels of the organisation. They command much larger fees as a consequence and their relationships with their clients last for decades. All of which makes selling much, much easier.

Your business environment

In-depth knowledge about your product and industry is a basic expectation in sales. Tech giants like Google and Meta put huge effort into ensuring their sales forces have in-depth product knowledge. They've implemented rigorous educational programmes for their sales teams, complete with mandatory exams, irrespective of seniority. These programmes encompass a wide array of topics from their core advertising products (which constitute the vast majority of Google and Meta revenues) to competitor analysis, industry trends, client understanding, pitch strategy, handling objections and more. While not all sales professionals initially welcomed them, the majority recognised how the programme addressed knowledge gaps in areas they didn't engage with daily and so increased their ability to help clients.

Let's begin with your products/services, your competition and your industry. The primary goal is to understand as much as possible about them all. Regardless of your field, you need a deep understanding of the product itself, its benefits and drawbacks, its applications, its structure. If your product is complex, spend as much time as you can with engineers, research and development specialists, and product managers to ensure you understand how everything works in detail.

Be a user of your product. This allows you to put yourself in your clients' shoes, sound authentic when pitching, answer questions accurately and handle objections. Test all the options, features, settings and applications – anything that can be tried. If you sell something that's impossible to use yourself, such as legal services or factory equipment, we suggest you role play with your colleagues, take the client's position and rehearse the sell.

As a salesperson you have to start by selling yourself on the product or service you are selling. If you don't believe in it, it will show. If you can't convince yourself, how will you convince others to buy something you don't believe in? If you are going into battle, you need to believe in the cause. It is imperative to be personally convinced, because much of selling is about the conviction you bring to the conversation.

Equally, you need to know your competition. You should know as much as possible about your competitors. Try their products. Complete their education and product certification, if available. Know all the differences, advantages and disadvantages compared to your product. Be informed about their value proposition, pitching approach, news and updates. Don't just research your direct rivals. Ask yourself what products or services your potential clients use instead of yours. How do they currently meet their needs? If you sell a service, you may want to focus more on how it is different from your competitors and better understand not *what* you do but *how* you do it. A lot of businesses offer the same services if we start explaining what they do – e.g. real estate agents all sell and lease property, attorneys provide commercial services, conveyancing, family law, last wills and testaments, and accountants all sell auditing, tax planning and bookkeeping. However, each provider can have a different value proposition because each may target different clients geographically, specialise in different areas of competence or on specific industries and types of clients.

Once you've done all this and have a comprehensive view of where you stand against your direct and indirect competitors, make a positioning map.

Without getting all 'business-schooly' about it, positioning maps are commonly used in marketing. They help you see the dynamics in your market and the key attributes that drive that market. Plot your competitors on the axes which you feel represent the way the market works. Here are several examples: speed of service versus quality; price versus brand reputation; technological sophistication versus user-friendliness; innovation versus customer experience.

Have a close look at your competitors' websites and see how they talk about themselves. It is likely that they all use similar language in their sales and marketing efforts – this is the way they think and talk about themselves. Very often you will be able to find similarities. For instance, we found that most consultancies talk a lot about themselves – what they do and how they do it – as well as how they achieve great results (perceived client benefits). But very few of them talked about the clients themselves and what role those achievements will play in the client's life. Plotting this on a positioning map identified a gap in the market.

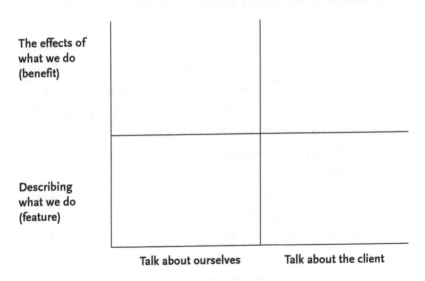

Your client's business

The highest compliment a client can pay you is to say, 'You really understand my business'. It is a key characteristic of any trusted advisor that they understand how their clients make money, from their logistics, operations, supply chain, financials (religiously read the financial press and your clients' quarterly or half-yearly results), production economics, channels to market, investment strategy, policies, business strategy, board composition, key suppliers – everything, in other words, in your clients' world.

Why?

Because, to be taken seriously by your client in your field of competence, it is not enough just to be an expert in that field. You must also understand the wider commercial context in which that competence is applied. All the really first-class salespeople and trusted advisors on the planet make their clients' business their own business to know about and understand. That way, they deserve to be listened to when they speak – especially at the boardroom level, which is where we all aspire to be heard.

How do you get this knowledge?

If you simply bought a subscription to the *Financial Times* or *Wall Street Journal* and read them every day, and added *The Economist* to your weekly reading, you would be in the top 2 per cent of salespeople worldwide without even trying. These media are the most authoritative in international business and will keep you incredibly well informed about market movements, industry issues and company-specific news. There is also an abundance of information available online. If the volume of materials is overwhelming, use AI-based tools that can curate the information for you by summarising articles, picking relevant data and analysing numbers. This is where modern technology is so useful – it can do a lot of the hard work for you!

These are good sources of information:

- McKinsey & BCG articles
- industry-specific reports
- blogs, vlogs and podcasts by key opinion leaders (experts in the industry)
- annual reports and analyst reports of the biggest industry players.

Just as with your own industry, aim to be aware of the major numbers, trends, challenges and anticipated future developments. Networking, conferences and industry communities are other fruitful ways to gain knowledge, insights and data about your clients' business environment.

Understanding major market dynamics and the latest trends and innovations in your clients' world is crucial to stay ahead of the game. We work with a corporate finance specialist which operates in the creative industries sector. Although their core competence is finance, they have to be up to speed on the latest trends in marketing communications because they are sector specialists. They attend industry conferences, write articles about the latest AI applications for agencies, research the nuances of algorithmic science and read the trade press every day. All salespeople need to be up to speed on the world of business and their clients' industries specifically.

DON'T JUST DO IT, BE *SEEN* TO DO IT

Be visible. Attend *and* present at conferences. Join industry associations and be active in online industry discussion groups on platforms like LinkedIn. Write posts, articles, white papers and opinion pieces. Be intellectually active and physically visible. This will help you gain a solid reputation as an expert and will extend your network – from which sales will come.

Every year we attend the FT Weekend Festival. The *Financial Times* bill it as a *festival of ideas*. On stage is the editor of the FT, and you watch her and the top economics, political and foreign correspondents hold their editorial meeting to discuss the biggest issues and decide what stance the paper should take on them. All through the day you hear first-rate experts talking about everything from how to interview someone through to panels forecasting the next twelve months. Immediately afterwards, we summarise all this gold dust, add our own commentary and socialise it with our client community. As we saw in week two, clients are busy people so they're grateful we've invested time to anticipate the issues coming over the horizon.

Thinking and anticipating *on your clients' behalf* is what marks out the super sales performers from the also-rans. Horizon spotting is a gift to your clients. It is the gift that keeps on giving – both to them and to you. Why? Because the horizon is where all future sales come from. If you're too busy being focused on today's job, sales opportunities will whizz past you fast. Because the horizon approaches at speed in business.

There are lots of tools to help you analyse the issues facing an industry: SWOT, STEER, STEEP, SLEPT[3]. It doesn't matter which you use as long as it helps you to start thinking and structure your thoughts. We use PECSTEL, which is based on the PEST analysis invented by the Harvard academic, Francis Aguilar, in 1967. The PECSTEL process is a methodical way to identify opportunities for incremental sales to a client. PECSTEL looks at the client's business and industry from a variety of angles, so we look at their commercial pressures *in total*, not just through a specific lens:

Politics within the client organisation and world which impact the business

Economic viewpoint – the macro and micro influences on their ability to operate and grow, plus **E**thical considerations which are coming into play more and more

Consumer dynamics and behaviour, plus **C**ompetitive activity and landscape

Socio-demographic trends which will affect the business

Technology – the impact of technological change on the clients' businesses

---

[3] SWOT = Strengths, Weaknesses, Opportunities, Threats.
STEER = Socio-political, Technological, Economic, Ecological and Regulatory.
STEEP = Social, Technological, Economic, Environmental and Political.
SLEPT = Social, Legal, Environmental, Political, Technological.

Environmental pressures that will have a bearing on financial performance

Legislation that will affect the clients' ability to do business.

Using this framework speeds up your ability to disaggregate all the business pressures that your client is facing. Now you need to tell them the good news and bad news in person.

PACKAGING YOUR THINKING

Just as it's important to dedicate time to focus on the deep work, it is equally important to diary time with your most senior client to *share the results of that deep work*. If you've gone to the effort of thinking about the issues your client needs to be anticipating and if you've come up with potential solutions to them, then you need a meeting with your most senior clients dedicated to discussing them and all the long-term strategic implications.

We suggest you aim to diary a strategic meeting to discuss your analysis *three times per year*. Twice at minimum. They should be diaried and written two to three months in advance and given a title commensurate with their importance to you and the client. Call them 'Strategic summits', for example.

Crucially, they must be rehearsed *three times* (including a full dress rehearsal with a very senior member of your organisation role-playing the client) before the actual face-to-face with the senior clients. One of you can be the seller, the other the client, then switch roles. If you're alone, practise with an AI platform like ChatGPT. You pitch, and the AI poses as the client, asks questions and provides feedback.

The main thing is: rehearse. It's the best way to ensure you are prepared properly and it is also a brilliant way to develop the skills of your team. No one likes rehearsing in front of their colleagues. But those that do win more business. Take it from us: we make our clients rehearse and they close at 80 per cent plus.

All your hard work needs to be packaged so that you bring your client the highlights of what you've been thinking about. Whilst it is a discussion in format, it is a sales pitch in reality. The aim is to lay before your client the big areas for consideration and then give your rationale for which ones need the most immediate attention, in priority order. As you've done your preparation, you can then lay before them the options for proactive or remedial action, and present your ideas and products as potential solutions to the problems you have identified.

There is a useful structure for packaging your recommendations in this type of meeting, called **N I S E**.

News:

About your company that the client should know. Before you get into the main purpose of the meeting, it's important to update your most senior client about things they need to know about your organisation. Strangely, we only ever tell our clients interesting and relevant information about our company when we are pitching to them for the first time. We tell them about our history, our geographic reach, our products and specialist services, our values, our success stories – anything and everything to help them understand who we are and that they are working with a winning organisation.

After that, once we start work on their business, we never promote our company, show our passion for the brilliant work we do, never keep them up to date on new expertise or our own performance in the market. We should. Like all of us, clients like to feel that they are working with winning companies and teams. So this is your opportunity to share with them the highlights of the last four months. For example:

- awards won for outstandingly good work – ideally on their busines, but even if it's for work done for other clients, you're showing them your peer recognition for excellence

- league table rankings – to demonstrate that your firm is a player, a performer, and is seen as such
- new practice areas or new hires that bring new expertise to the client
- high-profile projects you are working on
- thought leadership articles and books you've written
- conferences where you've spoken
- your company's financial results.

Don't assume your most senior client knows all this stuff – why would they unless you tell them? Unlike you, your client doesn't read your trade media; they read theirs – and they're *very* busy people. So now you've got their attention, show off a little.

Issues:
About the client's business. This is the main section of the meeting. It's where you get to demonstrate that you've been thinking about their business in depth – where you bring your client the fruits of your deep work deliberations.

Don't overwhelm them with multiple issues. Edit yourself. Focus on no more than three big areas you've identified which need their attention. Then either ask them which issue they would like to discuss most (prepare to discuss all of them). Show them the details, the consequences for the client if they do nothing, and present them with options or your recommendation for what to do about that issue. You may not get a sale immediately; that's not the point. The point is to start the process of discussion and move the client towards taking the necessary action.

Ideally, you will walk away from the meeting with the client's authority to take the next step. A next step may be to do a feasibility study or to propose a test market or to write a recommendation report to present to the client's board or to meet with the client's commercial team and CFO.

Services:
That add value. Briefly, help your most senior client get acquainted with any new products and service lines your company has added so you can help them in new areas. It might be that you have a new research function or a new consultancy practice that specialises in identifying untapped growth opportunities in their media mix, or identifies ways in which AI can streamline operations. Whatever you have, if it's new and could be helpful, get it on their radar. It may not be relevant right now, but when that need arises, you want them to remember that your organisation is ready and waiting with the right expertise.

Extra:
Finish up with a personal touch. An invitation to an event; a book you think they'll enjoy. Do something which moves the personal relationship forward. We're not asking anyone to be obsequious or inappropriate. Just thoughtful.

You have to walk away with a follow-up action.
Conducting a **NISE** meeting will open up dialogue and the opportunity for the client and for you to ask questions. But this is not a debating chamber, it is a forum for taking action. *So you need to bring the discussion to an agreement on concrete next steps.* We have seen so many occasions where, at the end of the meeting, salespeople do not propose or close. They fail to agree on any real next step forward. Instead they agree to share the presentation and the clients promise to sleep on it and come back with their thoughts. They won't. (We will talk about closing techniques you can use a little later on this week.)

A very powerful way to get your client to see the need to act on the recommendations you have shown them is to ask questions. Asking the right questions is a special kind of art. Demonstrating genuine interest by asking open questions is key to understanding a client's needs and identifying additional challenges that you haven't initially discussed. To achieve this, apply a bottom-up approach to questioning, expanding your understanding with each question asked.

A helpful technique for this is the 'Five Whys', which involves asking 'Why?' repeatedly in order to delve deeper, uncover the root cause of a situation, challenge, or move the client towards making a decision. You might want to use other formulations like 'Tell me more', or 'What was the reason for ...'

Here's an example.

First why:

Q: *You mentioned that you're considering cutting back on our training services. What prompted this decision?*

A: Our overall company revenue hasn't been doing as well as forecast recently. We're looking for areas to save.

Second why:

Q: *Revenue fluctuations are always a challenge. What does the data tell you about what's driving the downturn?*

A: Our customers aren't returning as frequently as they used to.

Third why:

Q: *Do we have any clues as to why they might be looking elsewhere or where they're going?*

A: Customer surveys indicate they're not too pleased with our customer service support.

Fourth why:

Q: *What seems to be the challenge with customer service support?*

A: We introduced a new customer service system recently and our support team is still getting to grips with it.

Fifth why:

Q: *That's understandable, new systems often come with a learning curve. So this is what has impacted the client experience? How is it manifesting?*
A: It's new technology and our internal customer support team hasn't received adequate training on it. This has led to longer call duration times which means that other customers are left waiting, put on holding loops and get frustrated and angry. They either shout at our people or hang up and go elsewhere.

You: Would it help if we put a specialist team inside your call centre to give real-time help on site?

Client: Possibly. How could that work?

The process of structured questioning helps the client realise that something needs to change, that something must be done to avert disaster or capitalise on advantage.

The golden rules about asking questions:

1. Pose questions that stimulate possibility-oriented thinking rather than critical, judgemental thinking.

For example, begin with 'What if ... ?' or 'What else could we do ... ?' Choose open-ended formulations beginning with 'What...' or 'How ...' Maintaining a 'discovery' mindset can help you identify underlying needs or problems and broaden the scope of your collaboration – as in the example above.

2. Have a list of open questions and practise using them with a colleague before your client meeting. Go back to your 'library' of questions and keep adding to it when you find new ones that work.

3. Listen to the answers. Like a good TV interviewer, go where the client takes you with their responses – don't stick rigidly to your list. This is a sales conversation, not a script. It will have its own dynamic and will take unpredictable turns. Active listening is an essential skill in sales. Practise it. On your life partner. With your children. With your family and friends.

Stop anticipating their next sentence or waiting for them to finish so you can say what you want to say. Shut up and listen.

You will learn something. And your partner, your children, family, friends, colleagues and clients will notice. Which means you will get better outcomes. Ta-da!

We were guests at a conference for the leaders of a large international consultancy firm. The invited guest speaker, the CEO of Unilever, spoke in the final slot of the afternoon. He spoke about Unilever's business needs today and their challenges for the future. Being practised active listeners, we spotted nineteen 'needs' that the man from Unilever mentioned during his speech. All of which the consultancy business could help Unilever solve.

In the cocktail reception afterwards, we took the list of nineteen potential projects to the global CEO of the consultancy firm. He was frustrated. The conference that he had organised was focused on new business – and yet none of his leadership team listening in the conference hall had *heard* any of the opportunities.

Your internal radar has to be 'on' to hear opportunities. You have to employ your peripheral vision and hearing; not every opportunity that comes your way will be gift-wrapped or even be the opportunity you were originally pursuing. But if you are 'on', you will catch it. And if you catch it, you can sell a solution.

Structuring your sales conversation

A friend of ours has a garden. Her garden is on a slope. She wanted it levelled out so that she could put a table-tennis table outside for her teenagers to use. She asked three landscape gardening contractors to quote for the work. They all came round to her home to scope out the job. The first two contractors told her that they could do the job for £5,500 and £6,500 respectively and that it would take between seven and ten days. The third contractor used something we call the **FEES** technique. He established the *facts* by finding out what our friend used her garden for. By questioning and probing deeper, he discovered that she liked sitting outside and socialising with friends in the garden but that she wanted a low-maintenance garden because she was busy with work. A bit more than a simple levelling-out job.

The contractor asked if having two levels might work better. One for the table-tennis table, the other with room for a table, umbrella and chairs for when she had friends over. He pointed out that they could pave over the flower beds, thus making the dining space bigger overall, and use terracotta pots for planting to add some colour and make it all low maintenance. Nirvana. And a great example of how to find out the facts and *explore* the opportunities available.

The builder moved on to *expanding* her needs. He said he noticed what a big and well-laid-out kitchen our friend had as she walked him through the house to the garden. 'Do you enjoy cooking?', he asked. Our friend replied that she did. 'I notice that there's this small area to the side of the garden. Have you ever considered having a built-in BBQ there? It's out of the way but would make use of an otherwise redundant space.' And, he added, they could put some outdoor lighting into the patio to extend the hours our friend could sit out and socialise. Here he has clearly *specified* what could be done.

Our friend was sold. The quotation was 20 per cent more than the other contractors but, of course, she went with the third builder because he had (a) helped her discover what she really wanted and needed, and (b) the process he took her through had contextualised the price he ended up quoting. Instead of it seeming expensive, it actually felt like good value for money, given that she was getting what she wanted *and* more into the bargain.

The FEES technique

FEES. It does exactly what it says on the label – it leads to money. It is a process by which you lead the client through a structured sales conversation. It helps them understand that something particular needs to change, that the current situation is unaffordable if left untreated, and contextualises the cost of making that change.

FEES reveals to the client the actual monetary cost of what the current situation you have identified is costing them – either in wasted revenue (consequence) or lost revenue potential (opportunity). Which means that when you present your price for remedying the situation you've identified, it seems small in comparison with the size of the problem.

You lead the client through the four-stage process one stage at a time. Each stage is represented by a letter:

Facts and evidence. Present to your client the facts of the situation facing your client's business as you see them. No embellishments, no opinion, just the cold, hard statistics of the situation: loss of market share, increased levels of out of stocks, impact of inflation on their sales or purchasing, reduced margins, competitor activity, impact of new entrants into the market, etc.

Explore the consequences and opportunities. Here you demonstrate the cost of doing nothing about the situation you've identified, of letting the situation carry on unremedied. How much is the current situation costing your client's business? What will happen if it continues to get worse?

Expand the needs. Reinforce the need to take action by examining with the client other scenarios that will help them see even more opportunity if they act or discussing the consequences of inaction: for example, if the problem extends into other geographic markets or across other retail partners. Here you paint scenarios that show how the opportunity could be capitalised on if the situation improves or how it will snowball out of control if the problem starts to multiply across different channels.

Specify the solution. Inexperienced salespeople leap straight from **F**acts to **S**pecifying the solution. Invariably, this leads to rejection of your proposal. Without the other two steps – the two **E**s – there isn't enough price contextualisation for your client to commit to what might seem like a large sum of money for the solution. Clients need to be led through the FEES process methodically and slowly to get them into a state of readiness for committing to a solution that will cost them money. Don't rush this process or you will undo months of work (PECSTEL + deep work + NISE).

Often we come across poor sales skills in real life. Estate agents/realtors are a case in point. If only they would ask better questions to try and understand what their potential client *really* needed and used the FEES technique, they would be so much more useful. So many realtors just ask the client the perfunctory questions:

- What's your budget?
- How many bedrooms do you want?
- Flat or house?
- Do you need a garden?
- Area of interest?

They never probe beneath. They never ask the five whys? If they did, they'd discover so much more that could help them tailor a solution and win a client's instruction. And if they ever bothered to stay in touch once the rental agreement is signed or the property is bought, they'd remember to get back in touch when there was six months left on the contract to see if they could help that client relocate (thus earning more fees). Or stay in touch and check in every now and again to see if the property the client had bought was still adequate for their needs – people have children, so they may need more space. People's children leave home so they may want to downsize. You get the picture.

Closing techniques

What is a close? It's when you ask for the business or for the client to commit to a next step – forward, not sideways. It's no good to end the meeting by agreeing that the issues you've identified are interesting and to send a proposal to the client. That just kicks the can down the road. You're here to help. Helping means *moving things forward towards a solution* – not merely making your client aware of an issue. Making them aware of the issue is just the start. Your job is to help your client not only think about it actively but see it as a clear and present danger (or opportunity). One that you can help them address now. The most effective way to propose the next action is to say: 'Would it help if we . . . ' and then stipulate what you want to happen. Saying this is:

- disarming because it is non-threatening (you are only trying to help)
- powerful because it is a polite way to lay out the next step that needs to happen; and puts you in control of the situation and the timing.

Closing is how we get movement and momentum into a sales conversation. And there are myriad ways to close. But, as in all things concerning human relationships, some techniques work better than others.

All humans are born natural closers. Kids close all the time.

'Let's go to the park!'

That's called the direct close – here's what we want to do, let's do it. There are others.

The concession close: 'Why don't we go to the park for twenty minutes? If we like it, we can stay for an hour'.

The fear close: 'If you don't take me to the park, I'll run around all day inside and that will drive you mad!'

The alternative close: 'Shall we go to the park first or the sweet shop?'

The puppy dog: 'Pleeeeeeease!' With big, pleading eyes and the lead in their mouth! By the way, if you think this is just for children and dumb animals, think again: the 'puppy dog' close is the most frequently used closing technique on the planet. If you've ever asked a colleague to help you out at short notice, stay late or asked them to work over the weekend, you've used the puppy dog close. It's basically manipulation.

For some reason, when we go into business, we repress our natural ability to close. In our personal lives we continue closing quite happily ('wine or beer anyone?' – alternative close). But in professional life we shy away from it lest we be perceived as being pushy. Closing is the essential act of moving sales conversations forward. Without closing we end up on a merry-go-round of proposals which go nowhere. But how do you know which closing technique to use?

We've talked about the four different personality styles. As you'd guess, some closing techniques work better with one type than they do on others. Here's a short crib sheet to help choose the right one.

For people who like to be in charge and get things done (Drivers), use the alternative close:

'We could do x or we could do y. The decision is yours.'

It gives the power of decision-making to that person. And people who like to be in charge like to have control. Note: you give them a choice between two reasonable courses of action – not between an obviously good choice and an obviously bad one. People are not idiots.

For people who have a problem making up their mind because they always want to consult someone else for his or her opinion and reach consensus (Amiables), use the direct close: 'Let's get going on Tuesday at 9am.'

You need to help push these people to commit, which they have a problem doing. Speaking directly and with conviction might just help them get over the hump of indecision.

For those who like to dot the i's and cross the t's, the ones who measure seven times before making the cut (Analyticals), use the summary close:

'Let me remind you of the five logical arguments in favour of taking this course of action.'

This appeals to their need for thoroughness and myriad reasons that this is the right course of action.

And for those who suffer from FOMO (fear of missing out) and who don't really care what we do as long as we do *something*, use the 'fear' close:

'If we don't act now, your old boiler may blow up and cause untold damage to your home.' Again, be reasonable. Do not manipulate by saying something like 'this is your last chance' when in reality it isn't. Everyone hates manipulation – even the type of person who responds positively to disastrous or sunny scenarios.

The idea is to give the appropriate full stop to your sales conversation by getting the only outcome worthy of all that preparatory work you've done. Which is a sale or movement towards a sale. And if you feel that you are making progress in the conversation but there are still possible blocks or objections to the sale, use a *trial close*. A trial close sounds like this:

'If we could guarantee delivery on the date you want and move slightly closer to the price you want ideally, would we have a deal?'

A trial close is designed to test the water, to hypothesise a future situation where any objections to taking action are removed. It's useful to help your client imagine a situation where they can take action because they are mainly convinced and want to do this but still have a couple of (solvable) concerns.

SUMMARY
1. Make time for deep work
Do you spend too long at the work water cooler or checking out Instagram? Schedule time for deep work in your calendar for the next two weeks and find a place you really like to do it. Start with forty-five-minute sessions.

2. Audit your product/service offer

Evaluate your industry environment. Really get to know your products and services and those of your competitors.

3. Create a positioning map

Identify the key market dynamics that drive you and your competitors. Map your competition on these dynamics. Is there a gap you can occupy?

4. Identify the two main sources of information about your client's business, industry or the market.

5. Use PECSTEL or similar tool to analyse your client's industry

Stand back from the day-to-day and analyse your client's business through different lenses in order to spot the big issues coming over the horizon that they need to address.

6. Package your thinking using the NISE framework

Create space and time with your most senior clients dedicated to discussing the big issues rather than the daily running of the business you do with them.

7. Ask better questions

Use the five whys and other questions to deepen your understanding and, crucially, help your client to understand the issues and the ramifications for them and their business if those issues go unaddressed.

8. Structure your conversation around the FEES technique

Present the facts of the matter, help your client understand the consequences of inaction and show them any additional benefits to taking the necessary action.

9. Close

Sales conversations result in clients taking action on your advice. You need to steer the conversation to a concrete conclusion, not just end your proposal with a weak 'are there any questions?' The client must *do* something – otherwise it's all just hot air.

Week Four:
Art – the emotional side
of selling

*'The essential difference between emotion and reason is that emotion
leads to action while reason leads to conclusions'*
DONALD CALNE, CANADIAN NEUROLOGIST

This week we deal with emotions and the irrational side of human
nature. Make sure your internal radar is 'on' because it requires all your
observation skills. The good news is that you will have the opportunity
to practise the skills we cover this week every hour of every day. You
don't need to gather a lot of data, read books or blogs, have business
meetings or allocate specific time to think. You can start right now by
engaging with anyone around you, at home, at work or out and about.

The psychology of buying and selling

The premise of the Christopher Nolan film *Inception* is that dreams can
be deliberately constructed, manipulated and shared. This concept
creates specialists who exploit dreams – 'professional extractors' – to
steal ideas from, or plant them into, a subject's head. There are some
who believe that selling is like *Inception*: implanting ideas and desires
in people's heads to make them want and buy things they neither need
nor can afford. Ironically, this is the idea that's been planted in many
people's heads which makes them distrust selling and salespeople.

If the world really operated like *Inception*, it would make
salespeople's jobs much easier. But, thank goodness, the world doesn't
work like this and neither do professional salespeople. No one is trying
to hoodwink anyone or control another person's brain.

Human beings like to think that they are rational creatures and that when they buy something – a service or a product – they do so for rational, logical reasons.

To some extent this is true. When people buy anything, they buy it either to make a gain or avoid a loss. For most businesspeople, most of the time, they are in 'avoid a loss' mode. Why? Because businesspeople are often risk-averse; anything that manages the potential downside (avoids a loss) is most likely to appeal. As the behavioural economist Rory Sutherland puts it:

> You make the decision that's easiest to defend, or least likely to come under attack. In B2B, avoiding catastrophe is more important than achieving perfection.

Rory reasons that in a business there are a lot of things you could do to get fired, but not much you can do to get a £1m bonus, which explains why most B2B businesspeople are risk-averse – 'avoid making a loss' people.

Entrepreneurs are more often in 'make a gain' mode; they're actively seeking advantage in line with their vision and ambition. For them, the primary motivation isn't risk mitigation, it's upside. In an entrepreneurial setting, you can make eccentric decisions if the consequences will reap better results than no decisions. This is a 'make a gain' motivation to buy.

Your sales pitch must be couched in terms that will appeal to whichever mode of buying your client is in.

People justify with logic, but they buy based on emotion.

STRICTLY BUSINESS

There's a big lie in business which is best summed up in the line used by Michael Corleone in *The Godfather*. When Michael's older brother,

Sonny, tries to dissuade Michael from assassinating the police officer McCluskey and drug dealer Sollozzo, 'the Turk', who have tried to kill their father, Michael responds by saying, 'It's not personal, it's business.' If killing someone is not personal, we don't know what is.

We all pretend that decisions in business are objective. We do everything to demonstrate that actions are taken, contracts are awarded and sales are made on the merits of a rational case and in accordance with strict protocols of procurement processes. Bullshit.

Business is a uniquely human activity. Animals can invent things – several animals create tools – communicate with each other and organise themselves into packs to hunt together. But none of them have created a business yet. And AI robots are advancing at speed in their ability to execute many of the functions we use in business, but they cannot endow our interactions with meaning. Only we can do that.

As with all things human, business is full of passion, pride, pain and pleasure. The job you have, the status it conveys, the money you earn, the everyday triumphs and disasters, the relationships you have with colleagues and clients – these are all highly personal. Business is the quintessence of personal.

Which means that in business the personal touch matters.

Over the course of our careers, we have both turned colleagues and clients into friends. Into wives and husbands, in fact! Selling brings you into contact with fascinating people. Each person has their own fascinating story, personality and unique set of attributes and skills. Getting underneath the exterior facade of who we are in business *with* is essential to salescraft. If you haven't been invited to your client's wedding, you could argue that you're not trying hard enough!

Selling is really all about building the strongest relationship you can with another human being. A relationship of trust. And trust comes from demonstrating every day that you are in their corner, on their side. This means you are involved, invested in that person. So you need to take an interest in them – not just as a client or a contract number on a spreadsheet, but as a living, breathing individual. When you show up, they need to smile with recognition that here's someone who cares about them and gives a damn about what they're trying to achieve.

Get to know your client. Their partner's name. Their children's birthdays. Their own birthday. Find out what makes them tick, what passions and hobbies they love, how they spend their time outside of work. And reflect that knowledge by remembering when they have an important date coming up. Or offer them a couple of restaurant tips when they are holidaying somewhere you know well. Send them an article you've read about a subject you know they are interested in. Take the time to work with the person, not just the job title. And if they ever move on to another company, or retire, stay in touch. Don't be that person that only stays in touch because you want something from the other person. Staying in touch is fun – we still have lunch with old clients – and it often pays dividends, too. Many times they've passed on our name to someone else who they believe might need our help.

Building rapport and trust – Who am I? Who are you? Who are we?
Have you ever met someone for the first time and you just click? Conversely, have you ever met someone and whatever you try it's like talking to a brick wall – you just can't get through?

That's because you tend to gravitate towards and get on better with people who are like you. People who see the world the same way you do, who communicate like you do and who are motivated and moved by the things you're motivated and moved by. In sales, that translates into the adage:

People buy from people they like, and they tend to like people who are like them.

The first part of this sentence, 'people buy from people', is a truism. In these days of AI it's easy to forget that buying and selling are very human activities, as is business. AI can help us transact faster and more efficiently, but the initial buying decision, especially in business-to-business interactions, is between people – you and the client. Much of the time, they are buying *you*, not your product or service.

The second part of the sentence, '[people] tend to like people who are like them', is less well known. But we definitely find it easier to build rapport with people who are similar to us than those who have little in common with us. Which is useful to know. Because if you understand what makes you tick, you can also understand what makes other people tick. If you're similar to some people, it will be easy to build rapport. If you are dissimilar, you'll need to modify your own behaviour in order to overcome any barriers that might get in the way of you developing a positive relationship and which will affect the sales outcome you desire.

In weeks one and two we talked about our own behavioural styles and those of our clients. You saw that personality traits and behavioural styles may be very different in different people, which can cause misunderstanding and miscommunication.

If you are working with someone who has the same behavioural style as you, you will often see eye to eye and get on. If you are working with someone who inhabits a different quadrant – particularly one diagonally opposite yours – you may encounter friction.

Can you see how Analyticals and Expressives see the world in fundamentally different ways and how this will often cause conflict? For example, because detail doesn't matter to Expressives and really does to Analyticals, Expressives will not spot a typo in a document. An Analytical will. And if an Analytical spots one typo in a document, it signals to them that everything else in the document is suspect. Which leads to a lost sale.

Equally, when an Analytical insists on presenting fifty pages of data in minute detail, because they feel the need to demonstrate thoroughness, an Expressive will lose interest within seconds – they hate detail; detail is boring and unnecessary for them.

Having profiled herself and her partner, one of our Expressive friends says she understands now why her Analytical partner panics when she says:

'I *feel* we should do this'; or
'I *suddenly* have an idea'; or
'*Imagine* if we do that'.

If she changes the language to say 'I have been thinking about this for some time and we could try to do this . . . ' or 'Shall we discuss this and look at it from different perspectives?', she gets much more positive buy-in.

Another client of ours (a Driver) used to present new ideas in the style 'Be brief, be brilliant, be gone'. She was very sharp and always to the point. She often had brilliant solutions but was frustrated by not getting the response from clients she felt she deserved. She was really a brilliant specialist, but clients seemed to listen to her colleague much more. She could not understand why, until she realised that most people she worked with were Amiables. Her colleague was good at offering tea, drinking it with clients and chatting about life before getting to business. Next time, our friend tried a very simple thing – before jumping straight to business she asked her client how their day was and whether they wanted tea. She made one for herself, showing that it was sincere and not just a perfunctory ritual. She was amazed how much better the conversation went.

We hear similar stories again and again. People say the same things but change the style, mode and wording, and, suddenly, they are heard. Drivers want to be nice and friendly, too. Amiables can be decisive. Expressives can analyse and Analyticals express. We just do it differently. And if we understand each other's language, everyone benefits.

When you are selling as a team, you should aim to have representatives of each of the four groups because that will maximise your chances of finding a fit with your clients' people, who will also have representatives of all four groups. If you're only meeting one or two clients and it's inappropriate to turn up mob-handed, don't panic. The truth is, everyone has *some* of the qualities of each of the four personality styles. Just make sure your internal radar is switched on. When you meet your clients, adapt your own behaviour to shift slightly into a different mode once you've worked out what personality style you are dealing with – slow down, speed up, keep it topline or ask if they'd like to drill down into the details a little more.

HOW DO YOU BEHAVE ONCE YOU KNOW WHO IS IN FRONT OF YOU?

If you really haven't got a clue who is going to turn up to your sales meeting (and you should, because you should have done your homework), assume they are Amiable at first. That way you have the least risk of offending the person within the first few minutes. You will quickly spot who you are dealing with and be able to adapt your behaviour and language accordingly to achieve the best fit and build rapport between you both.

Often, getting the best out of someone else means avoiding the things that irritate them. So:

For Analyticals:
- Talk calmly; don't be loud or flamboyant.
- Send them an agenda in advance.
- Stick to the facts; don't share unsubstantiated personal opinions and don't be spontaneous with them. You will make them feel unprepared. Never throw a surprise birthday party for an Analytical person. They hate surprises.
- Use evidence to validate your case.
- Don't make mistakes (check every letter of every word and every column of figures in your document). If they spot one mistake, it will make them suspect everything else you say.

- Use language in a structured way to signal ordered thought. For example, say 'firstly; secondly; thirdly'.
- Use words such as plan, strategy, stepping stones – they signal thinking before acting and moving gradually rather than in leaps and bounds.

For Drivers:

- Don't waste their time. Be brief, be brilliant, be gone.
- Do your homework in advance – they will expect you to know a lot about them.
- Manage their time responsibly; they are busy and hate wasting time.
- Listen intently when they speak, and write down what they say.
- Never put too many words in your presentations. They will only read headlines, so make sure that your headlines deliver the points you are making.
- Do not disagree with them. Posit alternatives but never confront their opinion.
- Be early for the meeting, online or offline. Don't ever keep them waiting.
- Have a timeline for decision making and be decisive.
- Language: must, want, goals, achievements, action.

For Amiables:

- Be courteous and kind. Amiables do not like people who are unheedful of others' needs.
- They do not like to give bad news and they avoid conflict.
- They won't appreciate you 'railroading' them, and although they will probably acquiesce in the short term, they will find an opportunity to take revenge. You won't see it coming and you won't know it was them. They are very effective silent assassins.

- They appreciate teamwork rather than ego – talk about 'us' and 'we', not 'I'.
- Talk around the subject and about personal interests. Ask about them but don't forget to tell them about you, too. They need to know how you feel, and appreciate it if you care about their comfort, too.
- They like consensus. So get ready to get the opinion of everyone in the room when Amiables are in charge – even the tea lady may be asked her opinion about the company's strategic decision. *Everyone* has to feel good.
- Make sure the chairs are comfortable and so is the room temperature, and that everyone has enough tea and coffee.

For Expressives:
- Be positive, enthusiastic and 'can do' – these people hate negativity.
- Get to the point, give the topline, the helicopter view – avoid too much detail.
- Show them quick results or a route to quick results. They don't like slow progress.
- Language: lots of superlatives – give them the newest, the biggest, the best.
- Make your interaction stimulating and enjoyable. Think about where you are meeting and make it work for them. Dry, anonymous meeting rooms turn off these people. They respond to colour, vibrancy and atmosphere. Make your meeting stimulating for them.
- Ask their opinion and hear it out. It'll take a while, but they need to feel heard and appreciated.

Do all of this and your sales results will go through the roof. Just you see.

Overcoming client objections

Wouldn't it be wonderful if you did your deep work, used PECSTEL, set up your client meeting, went through the NISE agenda, went through your FEES process, proposed your next action by asking, 'Would it help if we started on the first of next month?' and the client just said, 'Yes!'

In reality, the sales process is often circuitous rather than linear. These techniques will definitely speed it all up and give you a much better structure with which to steer the process to conclusion. But clients can be mercurial, they can present different personality styles with different decision-making approaches. And clients might have to make decisions, especially investment decisions which involve money, in collaboration with other colleagues – procurement, finance, operations, the board.

All of which means that you'll encounter objections along the path to a sale. Objections are as natural as breathing. Inevitably, in discussing issues and options, you will encounter some resistance.

All too often, we take objections personally and emotionally. Which is why we are covering them here, in the week we focus on the role of emotion in selling. In truth, handling objections is both emotional and rational – but in the heat of the sales pitch, they can feel really personal.

The best way to handle objections is to anticipate and prepare for them. People often fail to do this. They rehearse their sales pitch, but they don't rehearse answering the inevitable objections that will be thrown at them by 99 per cent of clients. After you have rehearsed your pitch, anticipate all the objections the client could raise and formulate your responses. Then practise doing it. If you rehearse your answers to objections, you will go into the meeting calm and collected and with just the right mental attitude.

Objections often come at us as vague generalities, often as statements:

- It's too expensive (compared to what?!)
- I'm not convinced (which particular part?)

Our job is to stay calm, rational, objective and 'in state' (positive and proactive). *Do not fight.* Objections are your opportunity to learn more and demonstrate to the client that you hear them and are prepared to find the best solution for them.

Repeat the objection back to the client. This has four benefits:

- It reassures the client they have been heard.
- It buys you time to formulate your answer.
- You might have misunderstood the objection, so it's always helpful to check.
- If the objection is unreasonable, it also gets the client to hear that unreasonableness out loud. Quite often, when they hear you restate the objection, they might back off it or rephrase it or dilute it. People don't usually want to appear aggressive. They might simply be feeling insecure, or there might be something else bothering them that lies behind their objection. Clarify the objection and keep probing.

For example, here's an objection we've all heard: 'You're too expensive.' Sounds final. Bad salespeople will capitulate at this challenge and either lower their price in panic or give up. We see poor salespeople all the time who say, 'We can't sell this in our market because the price point is too high.' The job of a salesperson is to make price *irrelevant*. The best way to combat a price challenge like this is to ask:

'Compared to what? To the cost of the situation we've just shown you, which is costing your business millions in lost opportunity and haemorrhaging sales?'

If you've done your FEES process diligently, you'll already have established exactly what your client is losing or could gain in hard cash.

If you've already demonstrated that the client is leaving 23 per cent of potential revenue uplift on the table by not acting, which equates to $3 million, your price represents *outstanding* value by comparison.

If the client challenges you with another objection, for example, 'We already have a supplier in this area', what do you do?

You ask who that supplier is. You don't deride that company. You acknowledge that that company is very good. (If you deride them you're basically questioning the client's judgement.) And you ask if it would be helpful if you outlined a few ways in which your company is different from the one they are currently using. Then you point out that things change and ask if you can stay in touch so you're there when they do change. Ready to help. Then you ask about the client's planning cycle and decision-making process so you know when a conversation will be more welcome and useful.

The point is, don't panic. Don't be bullied. Just stay calm and come back with a reasoned and reasonable pushback.

Clients can have no problem with you if you handle their objections in this way. It demonstrates you know what you're doing and that you are listening to them.

SUMMARY

This week was about diving deeper than mere words or reason. To tap into this richer layer, you must constantly observe, probe and process the behaviours, perceptions and reactions of others.

Here's an experiment for the week: try to practise adjusting your style to your counterpart. Practise it first with your family and friends, then with your colleagues, and finally with your clients. Each time you chat with someone, play a little guessing game in your head. Are they an Expressive? Or perhaps a mix of Expressive and Driver? Then try using some of the techniques we covered. For example, drop a statistic for the Analytical type, or sneak in a compliment about team spirit to an Amiable. Watch their reactions. Notice their response. Adjust.

Focus on your client: take into consideration their style. Don't forget what's important to them, listen carefully to everything they say – even those annoying objections. Because it's all about making them feel special and valued. Which is the key to lasting relationships in business, as in life. As the American writer and civil rights activist, Maya Angelou, put it: 'People will forget what you said, people will forget what you did, but people will never forget how you made them feel.'

Week Five:
Organising for success

'It takes as much energy to wish as it does to plan'
ELEANOR ROOSEVELT

Many fairy tales end with a wedding – a 'happy ever after' moment. However, we all know that in real life this is only the beginning of the story. The real story – maintaining the relationship day to day – begins *after* the vows are taken.

In this final week, we take a look at:

- how to organise your efforts to ensure ongoing client relationships continue to grow and thrive after the wedding vows have been taken
- how to be systematic about the 'fairy tale' bit of the story – wooing and winning the hearts and minds of your potential clients.

Growing existing client relationships
Winning a sales pitch might feel like the culmination of all your hard work, but it's really just the beginning of a potentially long-term business relationship. The question is: what does it take to sustain that relationship over time?

There isn't a universal blueprint for ensuring client loyalty. At the end of the day, it boils down to the efficacy of your product, the consistency of your delivery and the strength of your relationship. If your offering remains the best solution for your client over a prolonged period, and you remain their trusted advisor, there's a high likelihood they'll stay loyal. But circumstances change, priorities shift, new entrants disrupt, people move roles or companies, people get distracted by new, shiny suppliers. Everything changes all the time. It's the nature of business.

So what are the key steps you can follow to keep your clients close in such a volatile world?

KEEPING YOUR CLIENTS HAPPY AND LOYAL: VITAL ELEMENTS

Stay Innovative: Regularly introduce innovations, fresh features, new products and service upgrades. We live in a world where regular updates and novelties are expected, otherwise you become obsolete. Ensure your clients are well informed and up to speed on what's new (remember to use the NISE framework). Employ direct communication, events, or meals as effective methods to introduce your news.

Seek Feedback: Request feedback on both your product and service. Listen earnestly and remedy the areas needing improvement. Whether through dedicated meetings or client surveys, create avenues for clients to voice their concerns and suggestions. Make it routine – at a minimum, twice a year – for your clients to relay their feedback.

'Your most unhappy customers are your greatest source of learning'
BILL GATES

We particularly recommend having your most senior management interview your most senior clients face to face. From your side, these people should not be involved in the day-to-day of that client's business. That way, they are seen as impartial, and clients are more likely to impart useful and honest feedback. Just as importantly, experienced senior people will have their radar on and pick up areas of pain for the client. If handled properly, these needs will lead to new opportunities for your company. We know a consulting firm who have used their Chairperson to conduct these types of client interviews annually. These conversations have been the biggest single source of new revenue in the company.

Join everything up and take ownership: Be seen as the SPOC (single point of contact) or *prime mover* by your client. Act as a liaison between your client and all parts of your organisation. There is nothing more irritating for clients than to have multiple points of contact with an organisation where conversations disappear into the ether or don't get followed up or are duplicated, where invoices are inaccurate or where the left hand and right hand don't seem to know what the other is doing.

When issues arise, resist the temptation to pin the blame on some poor, benighted colleague in accounting. Take ownership. Assure your client that you are *personally* committed to finding a resolution. Demonstrating accountability and transparency builds trust and shows that you're genuine in your efforts to help. Even if you hold a senior role and the issue is to be resolved by members of your team, emphasise that you will personally oversee the outcome.

Make them feel valued: Every client wants to feel special. So, even if you aren't working on an active project with them, drop them a call or maybe invite them for lunch. Remember key dates – birthdays, anniversaries, professional milestones. It's the little gestures, like sending flowers on a birthday or celebrating a professional achievement, that often leave the biggest impact.

And if your client loses their job, stay in touch. Be helpful. Be a support and a cheerleader for them at a time of need. When they get a new job, they will remember your kindness.

Assess your client portfolio: invest your time and efforts thoughtfully.

We know you have a lot on your plate. Building long-term client relationships and accelerating prospective clients down your sales pipeline is a challenge. So it's crucial to prioritise and allocate your time wisely to yield the best results.

Reviewing your current client portfolio will help. Observe the amount of time you/your team spend servicing a client compared to the revenue you get. You need to ensure you have profitable relationships, not one-sided or servile ones. Estimate the growth potential for each client and measure the following metrics:

1. Revenue over the year
2. Year over year growth (YoY)
3. Client contribution to total revenues
4. Contribution to growth.

If you have more than five clients, group your clients into clusters based on their size, performance and potential for the future. This is called client tiering. You'll get a structured perspective on how to resource the different groups. For example, suppose you have twenty clients.

Tier 1: Your top four clients represent 50 per cent of your revenues with modest growth. Retaining their loyalty and satisfaction is paramount. Allocate about 50 per cent of your time to them and try to sell them added services with volume discounts to reward them for giving you more revenue, or success-based incentives so you share their upside.

Tier 2: These six medium-sized clients account for 20 per cent of your revenues and exhibit high growth. These clients are your best prospects for future expansion. As such, it's wise to assign upwards of 30 per cent of your time to them. Bolster their current spend with a 'test-and-learn' strategy so they can try out products they don't currently use at low levels of investment. Running smaller-scale experimental projects that could yield promising results can pave the way for more significant investments and extend your relationship with the client. Eventually you want this group moving up into Tier 1.

Tier 3: The remaining ten clients, a mix of medium and small revenue producers, contribute 30 per cent of your revenues and vary in their growth patterns. They constitute the 'long tail' of your portfolio. With these clients, the challenge is to avoid over-servicing. Commit the remaining 20 per cent of your time to this group, schedule monthly meetings and semi-annual reviews. Doing this ensures these clients never feel neglected but it doesn't cost you the earth to make them feel that way.

Strategic planning and prospecting

Think of yourself as a gardener, meticulously planning your garden for the upcoming year or even several years ahead. What plants do you wish to cultivate? Are you leaning towards trees and shrubs or lots of different plants that change with the seasons? Or a mixture of both? Do you need a quick harvest, or do you have the patience to wait for richer, more exotic fruits? Maybe there's a precise spot where you'd like a specific plant, but the soil there isn't quite ready. How then do you prepare it? And amidst all this, how do you allocate your time and effort, ensuring every plant receives due care when it needs it?

Strategic planning, business development, and client portfolio management work on the same principles as gardening. Strategic planning acts as the master blueprint for the garden you hope to shape. Meanwhile, prospecting becomes your method of choosing just the right seeds, setting the stage for the most vibrant blooms and the exact harvest you want to reap.

THE GROW MODEL

To continue the gardening metaphor, we would like you to use the GROW framework, pioneered by Sir John Whitmore in his book *Coaching for Performance* (Nicholas Brealey Publishing, 1992).

GROW stands for: **G**oal, **R**eality, **O**ptions and **W**ill.

It is as useful for existing client planning as it is for new business sales – so we have combined them both in the framework below to save time.

The GROW model helps individuals and teams pinpoint their objectives by letting them understand the current situation and context, recognising the challenges and defining the desired outcome. Here's a suggested list of questions and discussion points that could guide your thinking or a group discussion about sales growth and prospecting for the upcoming year:

Goal: what do you want?

1. Define your annual growth objectives for your top five existing clients. What year-over-year growth are you aiming for?

Existing clients:

A _____

B _____

C _____

D _____

E _____

2. Identify specific expansion opportunities within existing clients. Which products/services can be upsold or cross-sold?

A _____

B _____

C _____

D _____

E _____

3. Assess the current client base and identify gaps where prospecting could fill them. Set the number and quality of new prospects to be added to your pipeline.

_____

_____

Reality: where are you now?

1. Review the current status with and potential for the top five clients in your portfolio. What's their current growth trajectory?

A _____

B _____

C _____

D _____

E _____

2. Evaluate your performance over the past year. Which strategies yielded the best results, and where did you fall short?

_____

_____

_____

3. Assess your current prospecting pipeline. How robust is it? (What amount of revenue forecast is over 50 per cent likely?) What's your conversion run rate? (How many opportunities have you won out of the total amount available?) _____

_____

_____

Options: what could you do?

1. Develop growth strategies for each tier group of clients in your portfolio. This could be based on deepening relationships, offering complimentary services, or addressing their evolving needs.

Tier 1 _____

Tier 2 _____

Tier 3 _____

2. Identify training or resources that you or your sales team might require to bolster their relationship-building, product knowledge or sales skills.

_____

_____

_____

3. Explore your communication and channels to market to enrich your pipeline. Could organising industry events, networking or targeted content marketing be effective? What approaches can you make to different prospects? Identify three initiatives to try.

1/ _____

2/ _____

3/ _____

Will: what will you do?

1. Collaborate with key stakeholders within your top five client organisations to co-create and commit to a growth plan. (Consider doing workshops, regular check-ins, or setting mutual milestones.)

2. Craft a clear action plan for the next sixty days which outlines how to realise both existing client growth and prospecting goals.

Action plan:

_____

_____

_____

_____

_____

_____

_____

_____

_____

3. Regularly review and refine the plan based on feedback, shifting market conditions or internal business developments. This ensures the strategy remains agile and responsive. Schedule periodic reviews specifically centred on prospecting efforts to grasp what's effective and pinpoint areas needing adjustment.

When used as the foundation for middle and long-term strategic planning sessions (spanning six months or more), the GROW model is an excellent tool for distilling the context, strategic vectors and desired outcomes. This will then serve as a solid basis for any concrete sales activities, guiding both your thinking and actions.

THE SALES PIPELINE

You need to manage the sales process for both existing and new client prospects in a structured, goal-focused way rather than just going with the flow. The sales pipeline is the tool that allows you to do just that.

A sales pipeline is a visual representation of where your prospects are in the sales cycle. As your prospects move through your sales pipeline, you move a deal from start to close. You forecast the revenue at the same time, which determines the health of your business.

Your sales pipeline will be unique, but it should still be reflective of the typical buyer's journey:

- Prospecting/networking
- Lead qualification
- Request for proposal/demo meeting
- Pitch/proposal
- Negotiating
- Commitment/closing.

Assign a probability percentage for each of the stages above and apply it to the deal value $ at each stage. Across all your sales activity this will show you how many deals you have in the pipeline and how much they could be worth at each stage of their journey down the pipeline.

You can create your pipeline manually, using tools like Google Sheets or Excel. Alternatively, software providers like Salesforce, HubSpot or Microsoft Dynamics are equipped with sales pipeline features.

Set up your pipeline this week and make updating it as routine as your morning coffee. Working with the pipeline will become much more intuitive when you use it in pursuit of a clear sales strategy and fill it with the right prospects.

Wooing and winning the hearts and minds of potential clients

Filling your pipeline with the right prospects means you need to be proactive, not passive. If you are passive and just wait to see which new clients come knocking on your door, you're not in control of who you work with. Too many companies are passive when it comes to selling themselves. They wait for the business to come to them. When they get bought by private equity firms who want to triple the return on their investment in three years, suddenly these passive firms have to get active! Don't wait until you have to go out and prospect for business. Do it now. Do it every day.

'If tomorrow fails to arrive, you must go and fetch it'
ZULU NATION SAYING

Business needs to be stirred up and chased down. You need to be networking in the right places and starting new relationships every day – online, in person at events and in the media.

But all this activity isn't worth anything unless it's organised. Sales prospecting must, above all else, be systematic. It requires discipline. Sounds like fun, eh? Okay, not everyone loves routine or process. But even the brilliant amongst us can't just rely on sporadic moments of frenzied activity. Every sales effort needs to be done consistently (every day) and methodically – the aim being to move clients further down the pipeline to a closed sale.

USE ALL THE RESOURCES AVAILABLE TO YOU

Sales is not a department – it is a mindset. It works best when it harnesses all the allies you have, both inside and outside your own organisation. Your data specialists may or may not be the most charismatic presenters, but whatever they are they can unlock insights out of endless columns of figures. Product designers may use technical jargon, but they can also help clients to understand what's really clever and useful about the new innovative feature they've added. Accountants may not bring alive the creative idea your designers have produced, but they can prove, in terms a client-side procurement person will understand, why creative design is more effective at producing enhanced ROI. All of which might help you clinch the sale.

Use the *whole strength* of your organisation's genius. Bring your product specialists, your data geeks, your design specialists, your customer care experts, your research department and your commercial team to help you demonstrate the efficacy of your product or service and how it will benefit the client's business. Do not fly solo.

There are other allies from outside your organisation who can enhance the sales results you achieve with clients and potential clients. Three in particular can be brilliant allies:

1. Colleagues of your potential client whom that person trusts. We have won lots of new assignments when people we know in an organisation have been our secret salespeople, recommending us to someone else in another industry or part of their organisation because we have earned *their* trust. And because they are trusted by others, others hire us on that person's recommendation. It triggers oxytocin, the hormone that helps people shortcut to an easy decision because it is based on the trust they have in the source of the recommendation.

2. Your clients' other trusted advisors. Many clients of business-to-business services and professional advisory firms work with a coterie of trusted advisors whose opinion they value. Lawyers. Accountants. Branding experts. Realtors. Architects. Cultivate relationships with these advisors. You might be in meetings with them and your client. Don't see them as competitors for the client's attention; treat them instead as advocates and take the trouble to help them understand how you can help your common client. (And maybe you might be able to help them, too.)

3. *Intermediaries.* In some industries, intermediaries can be instrumental in the selection process by which clients choose an advisor. These advisors have an intimate knowledge of the market in which your firm operates and, because the client is making an important decision on a business partnership that may last a long time or is a significant investment in capital, they need outside expertise to find the best partner. Treat these intermediaries like you would a valued client. You need to stay in constant contact with them and ensure they are always up to speed on any information about your organisation which makes you a more desirable partner for their clients. And help them by responding to their requests for information super-fast.

Common to all of these is the necessity to keep well networked. It's a cliché to say that it's not *what* you know but *who* you know that counts; however, this doesn't make it any less true. Make sure you plug into all the sources of business that can give your sales the edge. Prospecting and networking feed your sales pipeline; they are the hardest to do for most people, but they are extremely important, so must be done.

Just as important as harnessing all your internal and external contacts is to make sure you're speaking to the right person at the client end and be known to many in the client organisation, not just one or two people.

No salesperson can afford to invest all their hopes in just one client contact, even if that person is at the top of the client organisation. What if that person leaves the firm? You need multiple contacts within the client organisation. Each contact secures your grip on the business and locks out the competition. Each contact must be made an ally. And each contact holds out the possibility of new work – after all, every client will have marginally different responsibilities, priorities and concerns, all of which they will need help to accomplish. Help from you. The more of them you know, the more you can help their company and the more work you will ultimately win.

Create a comprehensive client company profile. This should include:

- key people, contacts and titles, including:
  - indirect decision-makers/influencers (e.g non-executive directors)
  - economic buyers (the CFO, procurement, etc)
- contact details
- an outline of the company hierarchy
- details on the decision-making process
- the planning cycle.

And keep records of all conversations and meetings with the different stakeholders you meet. Share the information provided by all team members, whether they work directly or indirectly with the client. A multitude of digital tools can help sales teams to maintain comprehensive shared records about clients (revenues, client meeting notes, client data, etc). Salesforce Solutions is a well-known example, but many other options exist. Apart from ensuring that all interactions are up to date and a record of decisions and ongoing conversations is kept, it also allows others to pick up the conversations and know what's going on if a key member of the team is away or leaves.

Meet all these people. Have a plan to ensure they know who you are, how you help their business and the results you produce for them.

And when you do meet someone for the first time, make sure you have done your homework. Prepare using open sources like LinkedIn, or gather inside information from their client-side colleagues or any colleagues of yours who have had dealings with this person. But do it intelligently. Too many people don't. We are bombarded with approaches from total strangers trying to sell us 'warm sales leads' but who contact us out of the blue as cold leads. They haven't bothered to find out anything about us or our business. Such people are in a numbers game – if they contact enough people, something will stick. That is not selling. That is throwing darts into the dark hoping you'll hit an elephant.

Be 'on' in the meeting itself. We recommend that if this is a big NISE-style strategic summit, go to it with a couple of your colleagues. That way you can split roles. One of you can be lead presenter, focused on delivering the presentation; another can be the summariser and chief observer, looking out for the clients' body language, ensuring your team *really* understand what the clients are saying and 'reading between the lines' of what is not being said; while the third writes everything down so there's a proper record of the decisions. Online or offline this is good practice.

Who can you work with or network with to help drive sales?

_____

_____

_____

How will you involve them?

_____

_____

_____

How will you meet potential allies and how can you drive the dialogue?

_____

_____

_____

SUMMARY

The final week of our programme is intended to give you what's necessary to get the most out of the time and effort you and your team put in. This involves investing your resources wisely, exploring opportunities and trying different strategies.

As you move forward, adopt the mindset of a gardener:

1. Observe and assess your 'garden': regularly analyse your current client portfolio and its performance using specific metrics.
2. Ensure your 'plants' are happy and well cared for: implement an actionable plan to keep your clients loyal.
3. Reflect on how you see your garden in the future: use the GROW model to plan growth strategically and plan tactically with a detailed sales pipeline.
4. Leverage all your resources to create the garden of your dreams: take an active approach to prospecting, partnering, networking. Don't just wait to see what blooms naturally, cultivate your garden with care!

Successful sales are like successful gardens – day-to-day discipline always works better than sporadic enthusiasm.

And they all lived happily ever after

Today we face an unprecedented change in how people interact with the world and interpret the whole idea of relationships, be that romantic relationships, employer to employee relationships, business partnerships, and even relationships between consumers and brands. Society is gradually shifting away from monogamous norms. Research from 2020–2021, conducted during the pandemic, revealed an eye-opening statistic: in countries like Sweden, 41 per cent of all households consisted of a single person without children. Meanwhile, Gen Z leans towards project-based partnerships and freelance roles with companies, rather than traditional employment contracts. The idea of lifetime employment wouldn't even occur to them.

Even in our everyday choices, we see change. With the overwhelming array of consumer goods and 'no name' brands out there, the notion of brand loyalty is diminishing. On top of that, many industries, from movie streaming services to automotive manufacturers, are shifting to subscription-based models: people often prefer to enjoy the benefits of use without the commitment of ownership.

We're living in times when people are wary of long-term commitments. It seems the age-old 'till death do us part' ideal is up for debate, both in love and business. What does this mean for B2B partnerships? And, more importantly, what's the plan for keeping your sales on the up-and-up and the cash flowing in?

In B2B sales relationships are deeply personal. After all, people transact with people. (B2B is really all about P2P – person to person.) We need to put even more effort into our personal business relationships against this backdrop of loosening long-term ties.

As we've said, business is a uniquely human activity. And it will remain so. Those who can keep the relationship growing will profit. Those who let it wither and don't spot the signals of decline will fall by the wayside.

We court, woo and seduce. Then we fall in love. Then we get into the mature phase of the relationship.

The seduction phase is exciting because it is high stakes. Normally, once we've met a few times and decided we seem to get on and that there's a spark of chemistry between us, we agree to move ahead together and commit. In business, that's usually the sales pitch phase.

Then there's a slight period of readjustment as we realise that from the inside of the new relationship things don't totally match up with the promise, but not so bad that we want out. We move on and then move into the second phase – being in love.

When we're in love, everything works and is easy. In client relationships, this means that the clients like spending time with you and hearing what you have to say. They pay your invoices on time and implement your recommendations. From your point of view, you really enjoy working with the client and you move heaven and earth for them because you want to please them and demonstrate to them how much they mean to you.

But then we reach maturity in the relationship. If we don't guard against it, maturity turns into decline. This phase is when familiarity starts to breed contempt, when weariness with each other creeps in. Phone calls don't get returned promptly. Emails go unread. Invoices are queried. Meetings are cancelled. It is the most perilous of times because this is when the relationship you have nurtured is most vulnerable. This is when your competitors strike, because it is easier to turn a client's head and attract them to a shiny new toy when they are feeling taken for granted by their existing advisor. When you stop feeling loved and appreciated and someone new comes along who thinks you are marvellous and finds everything you say fascinating, it spells trouble for your existing relationship.

The most important thing in this phase is to change something in order to put in a second phase of being in love. Salespeople and organisations which consistently reinvent and revitalise their relationships – by bringing new people, new ideas, new approaches, new initiatives – are the ones that thrive and engender long-lasting partnerships with their clients or customers.

Or you can simply wait for your prince to come along. But where's the fun in that?

THE END ...

THE BEGINNING

You're at the end. Which is the beginning of your sales success.
You have finished the five-week programme. We hope we have reframed what selling is and isn't for you, and that it all feels a little less daunting. Fun, even.

The more you practise the skills and techniques in this book, the more natural they will become and the better your sales results will be. Five weeks is just the start. In truth, it never ends. Keep going! If your internal radar is always on, you will spot opportunity *everywhere* because you are alert, listening and observing and reading between the lines with everyone you meet. And you are now better equipped to think of ideas that can help your future clients and customers perform better. Not only that – you can also *package* and *communicate* those ideas in a way which addresses both the rational and the emotional needs of your client or customers. All of which will yield you – and them – much better results. And with better results, selling becomes easier and easier until it seems totally natural. When it's natural, it doesn't even feel like selling (or being sold to if you're the client). It's a pleasure because you're steering your client to make better decisions which will help them change their own future for the better.

What all this boils down to is this: ***Sales is about being genuinely interested in people and wanting to help them.***

If you just do that, you're halfway there. If you can actually help them consistently and in a structured way, you will become their trusted advisor: one of those top advisors who whisper in the ear of the great and counsel the world's leaders in business.

Who knows? Even people stranded on a desert island might trust you now.

Index

'If, like me, you're the type who struggles to apply learning from business books to your day-to-day role, this is the book for both of us! A practical guide to selling in a refreshing, reframed way which focuses on how to build truly trusted advisor-based relationships with clients. A must for every client leader – I will be adopting it for all my teams'

Anna Hickey, Global Client President,
Wavemaker – part of the WPP Group

'This is a rare "how to" sales guide: one that delivers on its promise to help any seller – no matter how experienced they are – become better. It does so by framing the sales process as addressing fundamental human needs, then bringing readers on a discovery journey covering their own sales persona, the client's and the rational and emotional sides of the sales process. At each step it builds awareness and practical capability through simple relevant concepts, effective frameworks and practical exercises'

Guido Buitoni, Global Chief Digital Officer at Danone,
former Global Client Lead at Google

'Not only accessible and elegantly written, this book is also incredibly interactive and invites the reader to take a meaningful step forward. If you are looking for a concrete roadmap to sales, here it is! A must-read in today's turbulent and complex business environment'

Jeremy Ghez, Professor of Economics and International Affairs,
HEC Paris

'This book provides valuable insights, tests and fundamentals, but it also offers an enjoyable reading experience. I highly recommend it to anyone preparing for a crucial sales pitch. It presents an excellent opportunity to pause, reflect on your approach, and refine your strategies for success'

Severine Six, Business Director, Meta France

'A refreshingly different and human approach to selling, which anyone can make their own and which will generate results time after time'

Evgenia Brodskaya, Director of Business Partners Ecosystem, Google

'David and Maria have carefully curated a personalised programme of the greatest sales wisdom to help anyone be the sort of salesperson everyone wants to be – respected not resented'

Bruce Daisley, author of the Sunday Times bestsellers
Fortitude* and *The Joy of Work

'This book goes beyond traditional methods: it not only sharpens your sales skills but also enriches your understanding of self and others, making it an essential companion for anyone eager to excel in the modern marketplace'

Lino Cattaruzzi, Global Client Partner, Google